Your Retirement Benefits

THE ICFP PERSONAL WEALTH BUILDING GUIDES

Your Retirement Benefits

Peter E. Gaudio
Virginia S. Nicols

JOHN WILEY & SONS, INC.

New York • Chichester • Brisbane • Toronto • Singapore

This book is dedicated to all those who had the nerve to raise their hand and begin with, "I have a question. . . !"

Copyright © 1992 by Peter E. Gaudio and Virginia S. Nicols. Published by John Wiley & Sons, Inc.

All rights reserved. Published simultaneously in Canada.

CFP and Certified Financial Planner are federally registered service marks of the International Board of Standards and Practices for Certified Financial Planners, Inc. (IBCFP).

Reproduction or translation of any part of this work beyond that permitted by Section 107 or 108 of the 1976 United States Copyright Act without the permission of the copyright owner is unlawful. Requests for permission or further information should be addressed to the Permissions Department, John Wiley & Sons, Inc.

This publication is designed to provide accurate and authoritative information in regard to the subject matter covered. It is sold with the understanding that the publisher is not engaged in rendering legal, accounting, or other professional services. If legal advice or other expert assistance is required, the services of a competent professional person should be sought. *From a Declaration of Principles jointly adopted by a Committee of the American Bar Association and a Committee of Publishers.*

Library of Congress Cataloging-in-Publication Data

Gaudio, Peter E., 1950–
    Your retirement benefits / by Peter E. Gaudio, Virginia S. Nicols.
      p.   cm. — (The ICFP personal wealth-building guides)
    Includes index
    ISBN 0-471-53965-1   ISBN 0-471-53966-X (pbk.)
    1. Old age pensions—United States. 2. Pensions—United States.
3. Pension trusts—United States. 4. Retirement—United States—
Planning. I. Nicols, Virginia S. II. Title. III. Series.
HD7105.35.U6G38   1992
332.024'01—dc20   91-37446

10 9 8 7 6 5 4 3 2 1

Printed and bound by Malloy Lithographing, Inc.

Acknowledgments

*T*his is a book for real people; it originated from actual experiences. Our greatest debt is to all our clients and seminar attendees who, over the years, gave us the background material for our Wealth Building Profiles and our illustrations. We have changed their names, but their stories are real. We also thank the many companies, particularly IBM and Lockheed, that asked us to come to their premises and conduct seminars on retirement planning.

For technical assistance and critical review, we especially thank Jim McIlrath, JD, Mark Weimer, CPC, and H. Lynn Hopewell, CFP, who took their valuable time to review, page-by-page, what became a very long manuscript. Their expertise was reflected in their contributions, which were greatly appreciated.

For early inspiration and encouragement throughout, our thanks go to Joseph Bird, PhD, whose vision and expertise helped us to put our experience and ideas into book form. Joe is well into his own highly successful retirement career.

Finally, on the business side, we wish to thank all the people at John Wiley & Sons who helped make this book possible. The persistence and hard work of our editor, Wendy Grau, is especially acknowledged.

Because the writing of any book is very personal, we can include special thanks to Marge Strathman, who cheerfully gave up evenings and weekends and married Peter anyway; to Joe Krueger, who steadily fed us the writing and marketing resources that turned the whole project into a reality; and to our parents and children and brothers and sisters, who seemed to take as much pleasure from our progress as we did!

P.E.G.
V.S.N.

Contents

INTRODUCTION

*R*etirement. Not too long ago, the word caused a yawn, but not so today! More people are retiring, and many are retiring earlier—with hopes for a long and fruitful retirement.

How do you view *your* retirement? Are you looking forward to it with zest? Are you yearning to have the time to pursue your personal interests? Or are you among those who see retirement only as a time when income will drop to near-poverty levels, making a "gracious retirement life-style" little more than a dream? Whatever your viewpoint, these facts are critical:

▶ With today's trend toward early retirement, and continuing advances in health care, you can expect to live about *two decades* after retirement—as long as another career!

▶ The need for a well-thought-out and well-organized retirement has never been greater.

Retirement finances are only part of the picture. Suitable housing, time management, and the physical and emotional stresses of aging—all these issues must be addressed. Usually, though, the core of retirement security is sound finances.

WHAT THIS BOOK OFFERS

Your Retirement Benefits focuses on one major source of retirement security: retirement plans. Its purpose is to help you deal with the practical issues surrounding *your* retirement plan. First and foremost, we want to help you understand your plan's value!

The book puts you on equal footing with "experts" in the field, and it may give you ideas for enhancing or protecting your retirement plan that even they don't know.

One caveat: this is not a book on investing for retirement income. We deal with investment issues as they relate to your retirement plan, but we will refer you to the many other available resources for in-depth investment technicalities and strategies.

HOW THE BOOK EVOLVED

We first became aware of how little understanding most people have about the financial aspects of retirement while we were conducting "preretirement" classes. Most class participants, we found, although trained to work and *make* money, had little training and practically no confidence in their ability to *keep* money and make it work for them. We spoke with thousands of people. They all asked questions, in the classes and in private sessions afterward.

Over time, a similarity in the questions began to show up, from class to class and employer to employer. We began writing booklets and other study material containing answers to questions we were repeatedly asked. This material met with great success; it is now often bought by employees even without the benefit of a class!

Your Retirements Benefits stems from participants' questions during and after classroom sessions and from their response to our study materials.

HOW TO USE THIS BOOK

We have adapted our classroom format to the presentation in this book. On each topic, you first "listen in" on a lecture and discussion. As in any classroom, people have their personal stories to tell, and the sections entitled Wealth Building Profile show how real-life situations can be handled. Each Action Item and Worksheet will help you to organize your information, so that you can put *your own* retirement plan to work. You won't find the information in this book worth the paper it's printed on if you don't take action!

When you take action, count on saving both time and money. If you seek help from your employee benefits representative, you'll understand what your retirement plan offers and you can get right to the details you're seeking. When you must make investment or tax decisions, you'll avoid paying a professional an hourly fee for first educating you about your retirement plan. In fact, you'll bring a wealth of information and planning ideas to that meeting!

Even though this book is arranged to be read straight through, you don't have to follow that course. The chapters on distributions and rollovers, or those on understanding your particular Retirement Plan may be most important to you right now. You may wish to turn directly to those topics, saving other information for later.

Each chapter can stand alone. As you browse, watch for references to other chapters or to a specific outside resource that may be helpful to you.

In Chapters 6 through 11, you will find *Overview Charts*—handy guides to each chapter's retirement plan. They allow you to review major features and see how they change as your employment situation changes. For example, you can see at a glance how your survivors will be affected if you die while still employed.

A list of Points to Remember closes each chapter.

WHO SHOULD READ THIS BOOK?

Your Retirement Benefits is for everyone approaching retirement and for anyone with questions about retirement plans. No matter what your age or stage in your working life, this book is applicable to your future.

We hope our book will serve you in two very different ways: to *protect* you from serious oversight at each decision point, and to make sure, all along the way, that you *profit* from your own good management.

1

Getting Started

KNOWING WHAT YOU HAVE

*T*he day you retire is not the day to figure out your plans for retirement. If you were a theatrical star, would you wait until the very day of a performance to learn your lines? Of course not! Along with being the lead character in your retirement, you are in charge of screenwriting and directing, as well as lighting, sound, and set design!

Staging a successful retirement requires organization, planning, management, and practice.

This book focuses on one of the most valuable retirement assets that people have—their retirement plans. For all their importance, retirement plans are generally undermanaged and, too often, misunderstood. Because information can be hard to get and the impact of decisions may not be readily apparent, many people miss the opportunities their retirement plans offer—year after year, not just at the exit interview.

WHAT ARE THE OPPORTUNITIES?

If you don't have a retirement plan, you may be able to start one, giving yourself the opportunity to accumulate tax-free wealth, at whatever level of risk you choose. Not a bad deal.

If you already have a retirement plan, learning the rules and making them work for you may let you retire with more choices, or even retire early. That's not a bad deal, either.

Retirement plans may provide opportunities to reduce income taxes, borrow inexpensively, and protect survivors.

Our goal is to show how versatile and flexible retirement plans are and how they can be improved through wise direction and good management. They offer constant opportunity. Retirement plans aren't just for the retired!

LEARNING HOW TO HELP YOURSELF

This book is about taking the initiative, learning the ins-and-outs of your retirement plan, keeping pace with change and opportunity—and why you can expect exhilarating big decisions along with troublesome little ones. Putting the book's suggestions to work is a big step toward taking control of your future and firmly securing it.

Keeping pace with changes in retirement plans is no small task. Sometimes, just knowing that a change has occurred can be a problem. By using our Action Items for annual reviews, you'll eliminate unpleasant surprises and alert yourself to issues that have arisen and to opportunities that have occurred.

Don't let one reading of this book be your last investigation of the subject. As income tax regulations, retirement plan rulings, or survivor protection plan provisions change (every few years, at the whim of Congress or through a judicial decision), the answers you came up with earlier may no longer be appropriate. We strongly recommend that you go over the Action Items each time you do your annual review.

HOW TO GET HELP

You have already started getting help, just by reading these pages. Throughout the book, we tell you where to turn for individual attention, we prompt you on questions that you should ask, and we provide worksheets to help focus your thoughts. Yet, this book is only the beginning, and it's only on the subject of retirement plans. Successful retirement will be built on your estate plan, social security, medical coverage, housing, and a host of other topics. We'll alert you, as much as possible, to resources in these areas.

We pride ourselves in thinking that this is a complete "how to" book. We estimate that it covers 95 percent of all retirement plan issues. However, the very experience that gave us this information also assures us that no book, no matter how complete, can answer all your questions. At some point, you may want to turn to a professional adviser—an expert who gets paid for solving people's planning problems. The Appendix shows you how to find and use a professional adviser.

POINTS TO REMEMBER

▶ Take the initiative in understanding and managing your retirement plan.

▶ Keep pace with the changes occurring within your retirement plan. Set up a system that protects you from missing them.

▶ Know how and where to get help when you need it. Be sure other members of your family know where important information, including names and phone numbers, is to be found.

2

Your Retirement Plan

More than half of the work force over age 50 in this country is covered by a retirement plan. Some of these people, however, will never receive a benefit because they will not meet their plan's basic requirements.

This chapter reviews how retirement plans work. It covers how to qualify for a retirement plan, how money is contributed, and how your retirement plan builds future benefits, during the years you are working. It defines the key pension and retirement plan "buzzwords" that are used throughout this book.

Because the topics in this chapter build a solid framework, we suggest that you read the whole chapter before you tackle the details of your particular retirement plan. You won't want to miss its important information!

UNDERSTANDING RETIREMENT PLANS

When you attempt to dig your way through your benefits booklet in an effort to understand your retirement plan, you may find yourself slightly overwhelmed. This reaction is not surprising. Retirement plans have become increasingly complex and are defined with ever-more-specialized legal and tax jargon.

The extraordinary number of laws and regulations are there to cover all the special cases, but the average employee must deal with these same rules in even the simplest situation.

The trick is to sort out the basic elements from the complex issues. When you finish with this chapter, you'll have a clear understanding of what retirement plans are, how they work, and how to take advantage of them.

Let's start at the beginning.

DEFINING PENSIONS AND RETIREMENT PLANS

The terms "pension" and "retirement plan" are often used without much thought as to their actual meaning. To avoid any confusion, let's look at the difference between them.

A pension is a sum of money paid regularly to a retired worker as a retirement benefit. The payments, usually monthly, continue as long as the retiree lives or for a specified period of time. After the retiree's death, a pension may also provide income to a spouse or other beneficiary. A pension is one type of retirement plan.

Sometimes, however, retirement benefits are paid in a manner other than regular payments, possibly as a *one-time lump-sum* payment. This type of retirement plan leaves it up to you to invest the money so that you will receive regular income after you retire.

Thus, a pension implies a regular payout. A retirement plan includes *all* plans, regardless of how their benefits are paid.

For the purposes of this book, we use the term "retirement plan" to include all payouts—regular, irregular, and lump-sum. We use the term "pension" to cover only those retirement plans that pay a regular (monthly or annual) benefit. In a later chapter, you will learn about a special pension called an "annuity."

WHAT ARE DEFINED-BENEFIT AND DEFINED-CONTRIBUTION PLANS?

There are two basic pension plans that lead to regular income at retirement. The first type of plan promises to set aside a certain amount of money each year for your retirement. Usually, the amount set aside is a percentage of your income. This is a defined-contribution plan.

The second type of plan promises to pay you a certain amount of money at retirement. The amount is usually based on your salary and on how long you have worked for your employer. If your plan fits this description, you have a defined-benefit plan.

When you retire, the money built up in either plan is usually paid out to you as a monthly retirement check.

CONTRIBUTION RULES

A defined-contribution plan is exactly what it says—a plan whereby your employer makes a specific, defined contribution to your retirement account each year. The amount of the contribution is governed by federal rules. These rules also keep your employer from "hiding" money in retirement plans and from paying out huge benefits to only certain employees.

The defined maximum amount your employer can contribute to your plan is up to 25 percent of your income but not more than $30,000 in any one year. (Most employers contribute much less.)

There are two categories of defined-contribution plan:

▶ A profit-sharing plan *allows* your employer to make a contribution of up to 15 percent of your income. Profit-sharing contributions are optional year-to-year.

▶ A money-purchase plan *requires* your employer to make an annual contribution of up to 25 percent of your income. This required percentage is set when your employer starts the money-purchase plan, and it normally does not change.

A profit-sharing plan and a money-purchase plan may be combined so that the maximum of 25 percent can be contributed toward your retirement.

Under a defined-benefit plan, your employer can contribute enough money to make your retirement income as high as the average of your three highest consecutive income years. However, there is an upper limit to the income you can receive from a retirement plan. The maximum annual income from a retirement plan is $112,221 for 1992. This maximum changes each year because of inflation.

Remember, these are the maximum benefits *allowed*. Very few employers are able to contribute enough to retirement plans to give their retiring employees the maximum benefit.

Figure 2–1 compares the main features of defined-contribution and defined-benefit plans.

The important point to remember about a defined-contribution plan is that your annual income determines the annual contribution amount. The plan's value at retirement will be the total of these contributions plus the accumulated interest, dividends, or capital gains.

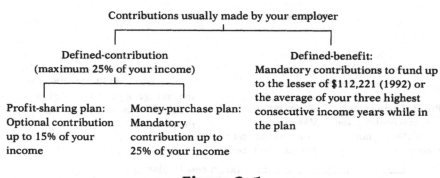

——————————————— **Figure 2–1** ———————————————
Retirement plans summary.

Under a defined-benefit plan, your retirement income is determined ahead of time. While you are working, the plan identifies a *specific* amount of income you will receive at retirement. From this, an actuary (a professional who estimates life expectancies) determines the amount that must be placed into the pension trust each year, to meet this goal. Annual contributions to defined-benefit plans will vary, because a better-than-expected return on the investments in the pension trust puts the pension closer to its defined goal. Future contributions can then be less.

TARGET-BENEFIT PLANS

An increasingly popular variation of the defined-benefit and defined-contribution plans is a combination pension plan known as a target-benefit plan. This type of retirement plan is most useful for employers who wish to make maximum contributions for older workers (usually the owners, or management) while still contributing to the retirement plan, based on a specific formula, for younger workers.

Target-benefit plans are closely associated with defined-contribution plans, as shown in Figure 2–2.

Target-benefit plan contributions can be altered, because a retirement benefit can be set in advance, as in defined-benefit plans. This advance calculation uses mostly an employee's age to figure contribution amounts: the older you are, the more likely contributions to your plan will be increased. Contributions to target-benefit plans, however, may not be more than the defined-contribution limits of 25 percent or $30,000.

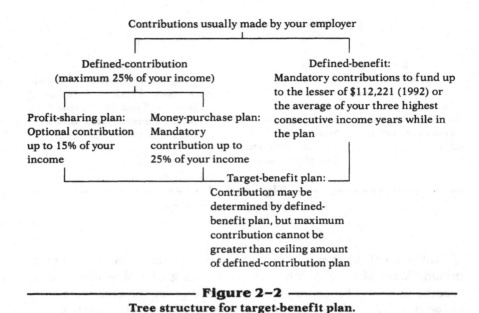

Contributions usually made by your employer

Defined-contribution
(maximum 25% of your income)

Defined-benefit:
Mandatory contributions to fund up
to the lesser of $112,221 (1992) or
the average of your three highest
consecutive income years while in
the plan

Profit-sharing plan:
Optional contribution
up to 15% of your
income

Money-purchase plan:
Mandatory
contribution up to
25% of your income

Target-benefit plan:
Contribution may be
determined by defined-
benefit plan, but maximum
contribution cannot be
greater than ceiling amount
of defined-contribution plan

Figure 2–2
Tree structure for target-benefit plan.

MINIMUM REQUIREMENTS FOR RECEIVING A BENEFIT

To receive a benefit, you have to be "covered" by the retirement plan. This means meeting minimum requirements, usually one year of service; age 21; and nonunion, full-time employee. Your employer must use federal guidelines to set minimum requirements in all retirement plans.

If you are meeting the minimum requirements, you are *earning credit toward* a retirement plan. Nearly everyone working for an employer with a retirement plan will be earning credit. However, that does not necessarily mean you will receive a retirement plan benefit in the future.

→ ACTION ITEM ←

Find out from your benefits representative the minimum requirements for being covered, or earning credit, in your employer's retirement plan. Have you met the minimum requirements?

Before you can receive a benefit, you must meet vesting requirements and you must reach your employer's standards for beginning a retirement plan payout.

VESTING—THE BASICS

Vesting is a schedule, set by federal regulations, that applies to your retirement plan. Once you are covered by a retirement plan, you usually have to work a certain number of years to "own" the benefit you have built up.

———————————→ **ACTION ITEM** ←———————————

Ask about the vesting schedule of your employer's retirement plan. Call your benefits representative, if necessary. The most common vesting schedules are as follows:

Vesting Period	Years Worked for Your Employer	Percent Vested
5 years	1	0
	2	0
	3	0
	4	0
	5	100
6 years	1	0
	2	20
	3	40
	4	60
	5	80
	6	100
7 years	1	0
	2	0
	3	20
	4	40
	5	60
	6	80
	7	100

Each year you work, you increase your ownership, or you "vest" yourself in an ever-increasing percentage, of your employer's retirement plan. After a certain number of years, you are 100 percent vested, or "fully vested." Recent tax laws have shortened the maximum vesting period from 10 years to a choice of, usually, between 5 to 7 years. Sometimes, the vesting period will be shorter than 5 years. Your employer makes the choice.

If you are working under a collective bargaining agreement, you may be under a 10- or 11-year vesting schedule. Your employer may choose a shorter vesting period.

UNDERSTANDING VESTING

Many retirement plans use the term "full vesting," which can lead to confusion about the amount of your retirement benefit. It may be easier to remember that full vesting occurs toward the beginning of your career, but you can't receive a full retirement benefit until the end of your career.

Vesting is directly related to the percentage of your retirement plan that you own. After no more than 5, 6, or 7 years of work for the same employer, you will be fully vested. Once fully vested, you can receive 100 percent of your benefit *at retirement*, but your benefit won't be much, because you haven't worked very long. Vesting, then, gets you into the plan and is an issue only at the beginning of your working career.

When you get ready to retire, at the end of your career, you will want to know how much money to expect. Here's where your plan's definition of "full pension" applies. To get the most money, or a "full pension" for your wage level, you will probably have to work 20 or 30 years *and* be a certain age.

WEALTH BUILDING PROFILE   *Almost But Not Quite.* Charlie is starting to think about retiring. He has worked hard at different jobs all his life and will soon reach age 62—old enough, he figures. Charlie takes a long lunch and makes an appointment with the retirement benefits people.

When he gets back to work that afternoon, he knows a lot more about his retirement plan than he did that morning!

He learned that he is fully vested in his company pension, but he won't get the full retirement benefit unless he works another 3 years. Why 3 more years? His plan pays a full benefit to a worker who has been with the company at least 30 years, or who reaches age 65 with at least 15 years of service. Charlie has moved around during his working years, so he will never be able to meet the first requirement. If he hangs in for 3 more years, he will meet the age-65-with-15-years'-service requirement.

Charlie starts rethinking his retirement plans.

 **ACTION ITEM** ◄

Review your current retirement plan. Get answers to these questions:

▶ **When were you first covered by your retirement plan?**

▶ **When will you be fully vested?**

▶ **At what age can you receive a full retirement benefit?**

SAFEGUARDS OF PLANS PROMISING A FUTURE LIFETIME BENEFIT

Each year, plan administrators decide how much money needs to be contributed, in order to meet future expected retirement plan payments. They make their decision based on federal guidelines that take into account, among other things, the number and ages of employees covered by the plan and the growth of the money in the plan. A plan that contributes each year, based on these guidelines, is "fully funded."

Not all plans are "fully funded." One year, or several years, could go by when no money goes into the retirement plan for future retirees. The plan then begins to build up "unfunded liabilities"—money that will have to be made up in future years.

Recent laws require that employees must be notified when their retirement plan has unfunded liabilities. Penalties can be charged to employers if they are not properly funding their plan.

Having unfunded liabilities is not necessarily bad, but the danger is that a company can get too far behind in contributions. In the worst case, the company could go bankrupt, leaving an unfunded liability, with no way to make good. The employees would simply be out of luck.

To protect against the possibility of having unfunded liabilities, most corporate employers belong to the Pension Benefit Guaranty Corporation (PBGC). The PBGC provides backup, to a maximum of $2,500 per month per retiree, when private pension trust funds cannot meet their obligations. The companies belonging to the PBGC pay monthly dues for this protection. If a company shows unfunded liabilities, its dues go up. The problem is that the PBGC, like many other large financial insurers, has only a small reserve compared to the total amount of money it is protecting.

Check the funding of your retirement plan. Is the plan fully funded or does it have unfunded liabilities? You'll find this information in the annual statement of the plan; you may need to contact your benefits representative to get a copy of the statement.

"OVERFUNDED" RETIREMENT PLANS

An "overfunded" retirement plan has more money than is needed to meet the plan's promises. In the mid-1980s, many plans became overfunded because the value of their stocks and bonds increased. These same plans today are at risk of becoming "underfunded" if the stock or bond market falls.

If a retirement plan is "overfunded," it isn't legally clear whether the extra money belongs to the company (and, ultimately, the shareholders), or whether it should be shared by current or future retirees. While the courts are deciding this, it seems better to be overfunded than underfunded!

WEALTH   *A Hostile Takeover.* Larry isn't too happy. Last year,
BUILDING   his company was unexpectedly acquired in a "hostile
PROFILE   takeover." One of the first things the new owners did
                    was to end the retirement plan, which was over-
funded at the time of the takeover. Now, they want to distribute the
retirement plan money to the employees.

Company news reports say that the trustees have set aside just
enough to meet the retirement plan guarantees. Larry isn't sure what
has happened to the excess amount, but he is definitely uncomfort-
able about having his retirement plan interrupted. According to the
company lawyers, ending the plan is legal, as long as the employees
aren't denied benefits they have been promised.

**I understand why I want a retirement plan, but why
would my employer give me one if it's not required?**

Employers give a variety of reasons for setting up a retirement plan. The most common reasons involve wanting to
reward loyal employees or needing a retirement plan in
order to attract new employees. Employers who make contributions to retirement plans can deduct them for tax purposes. This is a big incentive!

**What happens to the money contributed to these
plans?**

Plan contributions usually go into a special investment account called a pension trust. It is separate from other
accounts and is managed under special fiduciary rules for
the benefit of retirees and future retirees. Details as to
how pension trusts are managed are in Chapter 3.

**Do retirement plans for self-employed people and
their employees follow these same guidelines?**

The retirement plans available to self-employed persons are
known as Keogh plans (Keoghs) and Simplified Employee

Pensions (SEPs). Keoghs follow guidelines similar to those already discussed; SEPs operate quite differently. We'll cover each of these types of plans later.

Can I contribute to my employer-sponsored retirement plan?

Maybe! Some plans require employee contributions; others allow voluntary employee contributions. If you do add money, your contribution counts, along with the employer's share, in figuring the maximum contribution to the plan.

What happens if more than the allowable amount is contributed?

There is a 10 percent tax on excess contributions. You have 2¹/₂ months, after year-end, to adjust your account without penalty.

Why doesn't my employer's retirement plan mention any "monthly benefit for life"?

You may be participating in a retirement plan that provides a lump sum at retirement. Most often, such a plan is a money-purchase or profit-sharing plan, which allows a certain percentage of corporate income to go into the plan. Each year, the contribution will be different, reflecting changes in the company's profit picture.

Because these contributions vary, and because you will be responsible for investing the lump-sum distribution at retirement, these plans rarely forecast retirement income.

I have a retirement plan that is *all, or mostly all, my money.* How does that fit into this discussion?

Examples of this sort of plan are 401(k) plans, tax-sheltered annuities (for teachers, and employees of nonprofit groups), and IRAs. All of these plans have their own rules and regulations.

Decision making about these retirement plans is quite different from planning for employer-sponsored plans.

They require that you decide whether you want to contribute, when you can contribute, how much to contribute, and how to invest the money.

At retirement, you'll have to decide when to get the money out, and what taxes to pay, among a whole host of delicate and complex decisions. We will look at each separately, in later chapters.

WEALTH BUILDING PROFILE *Surprise, Surprise!* Bill agrees, reluctantly, to attend a retirement planning class at his wife's company. Bill discovers, to his amazement, that Marge's retirement plan isn't anything like his. She won't be receiving a monthly pension at all. Rather, within 3 weeks of retirement, she will be receiving a check in the mail, cashing her out of the plan, and that will be it!

Suddenly, Bill is struck by the decisions he and Marge will be facing. First, they will have to "guess" the size of the distribution and use that guess in their overall planning. Second, when the money comes, they'll have to decide whether to roll it over into an IRA or to pay taxes on it immediately. In either case, they will have to make investment decisions very different from the ones they've made until now.

Bill and Marge resolve to start gaining a better understanding of these issues. They worry about investing such a large sum of money. They've never had that opportunity or responsibility before!

POINTS TO REMEMBER

▶ An understanding of retirement plan "vocabulary" is essential. The list starts with the difference between pensions and retirement plans.

▶ Defined-contribution plans set aside a certain amount for you each year.

▶ Defined-benefit plans aim toward reaching a certain amount that you will receive when you reach retirement.

▶ Each year you work, you "own" or "are vested" in an ever-increasing percentage of your employer's retirement plan. Today, most employees are fully vested after a maximum of 7 years.

▶ You will receive a full pension only if you meet your employer's age or length-of-service requirements.

▶ Nearly all retirement plan payouts are reduced for early retirement.

3

Understanding Your Benefits Statement

*O*nce a retirement plan is established, your work is just beginning. Each year, changes that could affect you occur within retirement plans. These changes may be caused by federal regulations, your employer, or new vesting or accumulation schedules.

Some changes are subtle; others represent a major reshaping. In any event, you need to know how these changes affect you.

THE BEST SOURCES OF INFORMATION

We turn to different sources of information for all aspects of our daily life: dictionaries, libraries, cookbooks, repair manuals, newspapers, TV, lawyers, accountants. It is hard to imagine getting through a day without using at least one of these resources.

For retirement plans, sources of information are no less important. An enormous amount of reference material on retirement plans is available. Any good library is well stocked with books covering all the rules and regulations. What most people want, however, is a reliable source of information that is quick and convenient.

With this in mind, we have identified three sources of information about your retirement plan that you should become familiar with. Let's start with the source that is probably most available for you— your benefits representative.

YOUR BENEFITS REPRESENTATIVE

The best way for you to find out about your retirement plan is to forge a strong link to your employee benefits department. Use the resources that are offered: watch for and read annual reports about your account, attend special seminars explaining benefits and new procedures, and get to know your personal benefits representative.

Your benefits representative may be your manager, a specialist employed in the Personnel or Human Resources Department, or a union representative. If you don't have a designated benefits representative, you will have to look for help among the following other representatives.

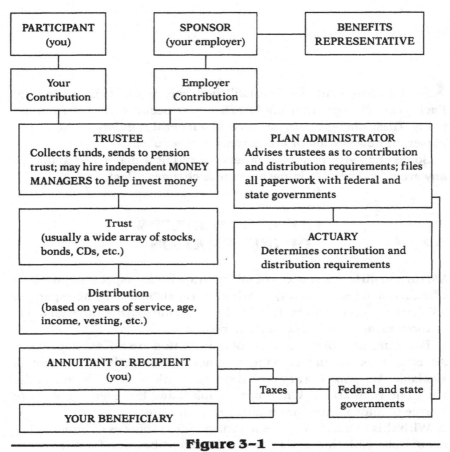

——————————— **Figure 3-1** ———————————
What happens to the money in your retirement plan?

First, there is the "sponsor" of the plan—generally, your employer. Your employer may be the federal government, a state or city government, a corporate employer, a nonprofit organization, a school system, or a small business owner. In some cases, your plan's "sponsor" may be your union. For our purposes, we will assume that your sponsor is your employer.

The sponsor appoints "trustees" to manage the plan. These trustees are usually people, from within the organization, who have the skill and ability to deal with the day-to-day activities and management of the plan.

For most plans, the trustees hire an independent "plan administrator," to make sure the plan complies with federal and state guidelines. The administrator may have, or will hire, actuaries. These professionals determine the amount of money needed by the plan to meet the guidelines, taking into account the plan's current and future obligations.

You are the "participant." (A retired person is a "recipient" or "annuitant.") You are a participant if you are building up *any* retirement credit, *whether or not you are vested* in the plan.

If you do not have a benefits representative, these other "representatives," particularly the plan administrator and trustees, should be available to answer your questions. Figure 3–1 diagrams the entire pension trust game. The players are identified in capital letters.

YOUR BENEFITS BOOKLET

The second source of good information about your retirement plan is the official benefits book or booklet(s) that you received when you began working for your employer or joined a union. Thereafter, you generally receive updates on an irregular basis, so your information may not be completely up-to-date now. Even in the time it takes to get flyers printed and in your hands, more changes may have occurred!

Use these booklets as a primary reference source, but be sure to double-check the accuracy of the information with your benefits representative.

It is up to you to take responsibility for getting an updated, complete benefits booklet from time to time. Your employer may not provide you with one automatically.

——————————→ ACTION ITEM ←——————————

Determine when you received your last complete benefits booklet. If it was more than a year ago, contact your benefits representative and get a new booklet or a complete set of updates.

ANNUAL BENEFITS STATEMENT

The third, and the most convenient, source of information is your annual benefits statement.

Each year, your plan administrator should update your record and send you that year's annual statement. Typically, benefits statements arrive in the first quarter of the plan year, and give information as of the retirement plan year-end (usually December 31).

Always save the most recent statement with your other important papers. If you don't have such a statement, ask your benefits representative for one. The benefits department may not be responsible for producing a statement, but your representative will know how to get one for you.

——————————→ ACTION ITEM ←——————————

Start a file for important information about your retirement plan. Find out who your benefits representative is. Ask that person to help you understand your annual benefits statement. Keep the name and title of the individual(s) and the exact name and phone number of the department prominently displayed in your retirement plan file, for your or your beneficiary's future reference.

WEALTH BUILDING PROFILE   *The Statement Wasn't the Whole Picture.* In 1991, Frank had been working for an electrical company for 5 full years. The company had a profit-sharing plan, which, according to his annual statement, had $15,000 in Frank's account, for his future retirement benefit. Frank wondered whether all the money was his. He decided to talk to a company benefits representative.

In his meeting, Frank learned that the company, several years earlier, had adopted a 7-year vesting schedule. This meant that Frank, with 5 years under his belt, was 60 percent vested: 60 percent of the $15,000 was his to draw on at retirement.

The following year, Frank would be 80 percent vested; after 7 years of working with the company, he would be 100 percent vested.

WHAT TO LOOK FOR IN YOUR ANNUAL BENEFITS STATEMENT

A good thing about the annual statement is that it is usually very short, often only one page. A bad thing is that, because it contains a lot of legal information, that one page can be hard to read.

The following Action Item will help you examine some of the basic information on your statement. Check this information for accuracy, each time you receive a statement.

→ ACTION ITEM ←

First, check to be sure your name, employee number, birth date, seniority date, years of service, social security number, and address are all correct.

Second, review the information regarding your life insurance coverage. Pay particular attention to the amount and type (such as accidental death and disability) of insurance you have. Be sure to remember whom you have listed as beneficiaries. Through your benefits department, make changes as needed (because of the birth of a new child, or the finalization of a divorce, for example).

Third, look at the amount of your retirement benefit. Compare it with the previous year's statement, to see whether it has increased and by how much.

Finally, if your employer has a savings program, note how much you are contributing and/or your employer is contributing to your account. Calculate how much your account has increased in value since the previous statement.

Most benefits statements provide information on vesting, indicate the earliest date when you can retire and your expected retirement benefits, and illustrate some pension payout options.

Look for your vesting percentage or the amount you would receive at retirement if you were to leave your employer immediately. Compare that amount with an "estimate" of what you would receive if you worked until your normal retirement date.

In addition, if the statement gives information about the earliest date when you can retire, calculate how much your benefit would be reduced by early retirement.

If you have a defined-contribution plan, your statement will tell you exactly how much money has built up in your account.

Your statement should tell you whether your spouse would receive any retirement benefit, if you were to die before retiring. This information usually appears in the "survivors' benefits" section of the statement, along with insurance data.

Don't expect the statement to tell you how your benefit is determined. The formulas used are often complex, and your employer may have a combination of retirement plans that requires different ways to calculate your benefit. (Information about how benefits are determined is discussed in Chapter 12.)

?

When my employer puts money into the plan, where does the money go?

The money probably goes to a special pension or retirement plan trust that is separate from other employer accounts and is managed by trustees. The trustees must follow strict rules (called fiduciary rules) regarding how the money is to be invested. If the trust is small, the trustees may do the investing themselves. Large trusts often hire independent money managers to do the investing.

Trust managers invest in stocks, bonds, government securities, or bank deposits. A small percentage of the money may be invested in the company's own stock. Sometimes, the trust managers invest a portion in real estate or in natural resources such as oil and gas.

If the money does not go to a special trust or trustee, your employer is probably purchasing individual "annuity" contracts, for which no trustee is required.

Can my employer purchase life and health insurance benefits with retirement plan money?

The trust managers of defined-benefit, defined-contribution, and employee stock option plans can purchase a limited amount of insurance for plan participants. This insurance benefit must be "incidental" to the primary purpose of the plan, which is to provide retirement benefits. The term "incidental" generally means that no more than 25 percent of annual plan contributions go toward insurance premiums.

How does my employer know how much money to put into the plan?

Under a defined-benefit plan, each year the plan administrator measures the previous year's investment results. With this information and the estimated number of people retiring, an actuary can determine the annual contribution needed to fund your (and every participant's) future retirement income.

The contribution to a defined-contribution plan is based on the current year's income or profits, according to a formula.

Can I tell from my benefits statement whether the plan is doing okay?

No. To find out about the performance of your plan, you must see the in-depth report about your plan filed with the federal government each year (Form 5500). To receive a copy, ask your plan administrator. This report is different from the personalized annual statement we referred to previously.

I expect a monthly retirement check. There is a large number on my statement, labeled "equivalent amount." What does that mean?

The value of your monthly retirement income can be expressed another way—as a lump-sum amount of money.

When invested, this money would pay you the same amount of income each month as you would have received from the plan. Often, the plan administrator will put this equivalent amount on your statement, to give you an idea of the amount of money working for you behind the scenes.

If your statement shows an equivalent amount, it doesn't necessarily mean that the entire sum will be available at one time *instead of* via monthly retirement checks. Some plans do offer a lump-sum choice, but your statement should make it very clear whether you have that choice.

If I have the choice of receiving a lump-sum distribution from my retirement plan, how do I decide?

This is not an easy decision. There are many things to consider: tax laws, rates of return, safety of principal, investment choices, and so on.

Most people are concerned with two major issues: how much monthly income they can expect, and how much flexibility they have in receiving it.

To determine the amount of monthly income you can expect from your lump sum, first figure the amount of tax you will have to pay. The remaining after-tax amount can then earn interest or dividends that will be paid to you. Unless this income is greater than the monthly distribution from the retirement plan, it would probably be better to elect a standard retirement plan payout.

In some cases, even if the income from the invested lump sum is less than the income from the retirement plan, you may prefer the lump sum because you will have access to all your money, any time you like.

WEALTH BUILDING PROFILE   *Change of Plans.* "With the money we get from the pension, we're going to buy a retirement home in the mountains, a four-wheel-drive truck, and some fishing gear, and enjoy life!" John and his wife Ellie grinned when they announced his retirement.

John thought they had done their homework in researching retirement life-styles. "We've spent a lot of time looking, and Big Oak Lake is where we want to spend the rest of our lives."

"There is a real sense of community, with a life-style I think we'll like," said Ellie.

A year later, John and Ellie still hadn't moved to their retirement dream home. "We don't have the money!" John exclaimed. "When we went to draw out our pension, we found we couldn't get it in a lump sum. It can only come out monthly!"

Ellie added, "Without that lump sum we can't afford to buy the house at the lake. We can't borrow money either, because our retirement income isn't enough to qualify for a big enough loan to buy the house. I guess we'll have to be content taking short trips up there in the motor home."

POINTS TO REMEMBER

▸ Your benefits representative is your best resource for up-to-date company information. Get to know him or her personally!

▸ Use your benefits booklet as a primary reference source, but double-check the accuracy of the information with your benefits representative.

▸ Each year, review your benefits statement for your estimated retirement benefit and for details of your life and health insurance coverage.

Government Retirement Plans

*G*overnment retirement plans may be likened to corporate-sponsored plans because they are controlled by the employer—in this case, the government. What makes them different is that government employees often have more choices about how much to contribute to their plan. This chapter focuses on those contribution choices.

The Action Items in this chapter are particularly important. There are so many different government plans that only the Action Items will help you sort out the details.

DIFFERENT PLANS, DIFFERENT RESOURCES

This chapter covers retirement plans sponsored by the federal government, state and local governments, and the military services. There are many different plans within each of these categories.

———————→ ACTION ITEM ←———————

Contact your benefits department or benefits representative and ask for booklets explaining your government retirement plan. Because this material changes often, be sure you have the most recent editions.

This discussion is limited to only the issues that are common to all government plans. You will need to turn to other resources to complete your study.

Start with your plan handbook. Government plans often have excellent handbooks, complete with step-by-step instructions for working your way through different choices.

YOUR CONTRIBUTION— THE UNIFYING FACTOR

Almost all government retirement plans are contributory. You must contribute part of your paycheck to your own retirement. However, different plans require different percentage contributions, and sometimes the contribution amounts change when new laws are passed. Understanding your contribution is the most important part of understanding your government retirement plan.

Most government retirement plans require after-tax contributions, but some consider the contribution to be before-tax.

Some government retirement plans may allow you to make an additional *voluntary* after-tax contribution toward your retirement. This contribution (usually a certain percentage of your income, up to

Do you make contributions?

```
                        ┌─────────────────┐
                       YES                NO
                        │                  │
               Contributions are    Check to be sure
                  /        \         you have a
            REQUIRED    VOLUNTARY    retirement plan.
                │           │
```

	REQUIRED	VOLUNTARY
What percent of your paycheck goes into the plan now?	_____	_____
Can you put more in?	_____	_____
What percent is after-tax?	_____	_____
What percent is before-tax?	_____	_____

————————————— **Figure 4–1** —————————————
Government retirement plan contributions.

a stated maximum) earns interest, and eventually can be used as a second source of retirement income.

Many government plans now feature a *before-tax* voluntary savings plan for employees. You decide how much to contribute, up to a certain dollar maximum stated by the savings plan.

To help you get a clear understanding of these potentially confusing contribution methods, use the decision tree shown in Figure 4–1. Check with your benefits department if you can't fill in all the blanks.

A CLOSER LOOK AT BEFORE-TAX PLANS

There are many different types of before-tax plans, and each has a different name. Your plan may be called a thrift plan, an employee savings plan, or a deferred-compensation plan. No matter what its name, most plans resemble either 401(k)s or tax-sheltered annuities (TSAs). These retirement plans are covered extensively in Chapters 6 and 8.

──────────────→ **ACTION ITEM** ←──────────────

If you have a voluntary, before-tax savings plan, be sure you find out its name and then read the appropriate chapter(s) in this book for further information.

▶ **Does the plan follow 401(k) guidelines for special lump-sum distributions? If so, read and follow through on the Action Items in Chapters 6 and 15.**

▶ **Is your plan a tax-sheltered annuity? If so, refer to Chapters 8 and 14.**

▶ **Are you unsure about what kind of plan you have? Check the rules regarding distribution from the plan. If you can choose your payout option, read Chapter 12, to learn more about your choices.**

The key to identifying which before-tax retirement plan you have is to know the way the money is treated when you wish to withdraw it at retirement. If you can use special lump-sum tax rules, your plan resembles a 401(k). If your retirement plan is not allowed lump-sum treatment, but must be withdrawn as "ordinary income," then your plan resembles a TSA.

WEALTH BUILDING PROFILE   *It's All New to Me.* Julie, newly divorced, sought a change in career in a new town. Her college degree and lab-assistant experience qualified her to teach high school chemistry, so she applied and was accepted as a faculty member in a state school.

Julie is now participating in her state teachers' retirement plan and is being encouraged to participate in a savings plan.

It takes her a while to understand the unfamiliar documents, but Julie finally figures out her retirement plan situation. First, the teachers' retirement plan automatically deducts 8 percent from her paycheck each month. This deduction is before taxes. The money is invested directly into the State Teachers' Retirement Plan Trust Fund. Second, Julie can contribute on her own to a tax-sheltered annuity (TSA). This contribution will also be before taxes. Julie will have to choose which mutual fund or insurance company annuity to use for her TSA. Together, her two contributions cannot be more than 16 percent of her total salary.

HOW MUCH YOU SHOULD CONTRIBUTE TO YOUR PLAN

Generally, your contributions to a retirement plan should be "as much as the plan will allow!" But there are some things to think about before you jump into a savings commitment.

Voluntary plans are designed for long-term savings, and they have built-in penalties for people who want to get their money out "midstream." Before you decide to contribute, review your budget to see how much money you have available for long-term savings. Try to earn extra money if you're not saving any right now! Next, see whether your employer contributes to your account. Some employers

---

WEALTH   *Future Value.* Barbara had worked for the Civil
BUILDING   Service for over 15 years when she and her husband
PROFILE   decided to move to their foothills property and raise
                    horses full-time. Barbara was fully vested in her gov-
ernment retirement plan, but she discovered that she had to wait until
she was at least age 62 before she could receive her monthly benefit.

Barbara had the option of taking out her own contributions to the
plan, but that would mean giving up the much more valuable future
monthly stream of income.

Barbara knew that raising horses had great business promise. She
hoped to be able to get along without withdrawing her retirement
plan money. The retirement plan checks would simply be more wel-
come when they finally did start coming!

If you have been receiving matching retirement plan contributions
from your employer, some of these matching funds may not be fully
vested when you leave. If this is the case, you will forfeit nonvested
contributions.

If you are planning to leave your government employment prior to
retiring, use the following Action Item to help clarify your retirement
plan options.

──────────────→ **ACTION ITEM** ←──────────────

**Review what will happen to your government retire-
ment plan contributions if you leave your employer
before retiring. Answer the following questions for
required contributions, voluntary contributions,
and before-tax savings plan contributions, if you
leave your employer before retiring.**

▶ **Can you take your contributions out?**

▶ **Will you get interest for the time the money has
been in the account?**

▶ **Can you redeposit the money later, if you decide to
go back to work for the government? If so, will you**

have to contribute interest yourself, for the time the money has been "outside" the retirement plan?

▸ If you withdraw money now, do you lose future benefits?

▸ If you withdraw money now, will it be taxed?

▸ Can you avoid taxes by rolling the money into an IRA?

SPOUSES AND RETIREMENT PLANS

Government plans offer joint and survivor payout choices, as described in Chapter 12. However, some government retirement plans are less flexible than others. For example, military plans may provide a 55 percent option as the only payout choice for spousal protection.

Before you begin a retirement plan payout, refer to Chapter 19 and learn how to use life insurance to enhance your retirement options.

WEALTH BUILDING PROFILE *Army Wife.* When Rick retired from the Army after 20 years, he intended to pursue a second career. There was no guarantee that a job would be waiting, so Rick and his wife, Jenny, were pleased to have his pension distribution begin immediately.

Jenny also expected to continue to work, but she had worked for so many different employers that she would never qualify for a pension of her own. She was concerned about how she would get along if something happened to Rick.

At the exit interview, Rick and Jenny reviewed the Army's survivor benefit plan. They agreed that a reduction in their monthly pension check was necessary, to guarantee future income to Jenny. Their monthly pension check went from $1,833 to $1,672, but Jenny could count on $920 (55 percent of $1,672) if something happened to Rick. The initial amount would be adjusted for inflation over the years. They felt comfortable with their decision.

→ ACTION ITEM ←

Before you decide on your military pension payout, review the survivor benefit option. Investigate other percentages, besides the 55 percent option. Be sure you calculate how much each different percentage will "cost" you in reduced monthly benefits. Read the complete discussion of replacing a survivor benefit with your own insurance, in Chapter 19.

Your spouse has certain rights within your retirement plan. As with nongovernment retirement plans, for example, if you wish to borrow, your spouse must agree and sign a consent form. Similarly, if you choose a payout option that excludes a spouse (such as the single life benefit), you must obtain consent. A former spouse may also have rights over your retirement plan, through a qualified domestic relations order (QDRO).

TAXATION OF GOVERNMENT RETIREMENT PLANS

To determine how much of your income from your retirement plan will be subject to taxes, you'll need to know whether your contributions were after-tax or before-tax.

After-tax contributions to the retirement plan come out tax-free, in the form of an annuity, or monthly payment. Most annuities are made up of two parts: the tax-free portion, representing your contributions that have already been taxed, and the taxable portion—everything else.

As of 1986, your tax-free contributions are returned to you over all your annuity payments. The basic way to figure your tax-free amount is by using the following formula:

$$\frac{\text{total contributions}}{\text{expected lifetime return}} = \text{tax-free percentage of your annuity}$$

The formula is not as simple as it seems. It requires using life expectancy tables (provided by the IRS) or fixed payout numbers

(10- or 20-year payouts) and making adjustments for joint and survivor choices. Furthermore, under a general ruling issued in 1986, if you outlive the "expected lifetime" and have recovered all your contributions, then all subsequent annuity payments become fully taxable.

Before-tax contributions are usually treated as taxable income when you receive them as retirement income. However, if your before-tax savings plan is a 401(k) plan, review Chapters 6, 14, and 15. If your before-tax savings plan is a TSA, review Chapters 8 and 14. You have a lot of choices!

If your plan is neither of the above, assume that your distributions will be taxed as ordinary income.

→ ACTION ITEM ←

Consult with a tax preparer, to determine the tax-free portion of your government retirement plan annuity. You may wish to refer to IRS Publications 575 and 721 on pension and annuity income or, if appropriate, the *Comprehensive Guide to Civil Service Retirement*.

TAX TREATMENT OF ONE-TIME PAYMENTS

Government retirement plans seldom distribute benefits as a one-time payment. However, you may be able to receive a one-time distribution of some or all of your own contributions. Your tax liability will depend on whether your contributions were before-tax or after-tax.

A one-time distribution of before-tax contributions to a government retirement plan will be taxed as ordinary income. You cannot roll these contributions into an IRA to defer taxes.

After-tax contributions will not be taxed. If the distribution includes interest, the interest earned before 1974 may be taxed under the special lump-sum tax rules. Interest earned after 1974 will be taxed as ordinary income. You may defer taxes on interest by rolling the distribution into an IRA.

─────────────────→ ACTION ITEM ←─────────────────

Consult with your tax adviser, to understand how you will be taxed if you receive a one-time distribution from your government retirement plan. Be sure you understand clearly how your retirement benefit will be affected if you decide on the one-time payment.

WEALTH BUILDING PROFILE   *I'll Take It Now, Thanks.* When Carl got ready to retire from the federal government, he learned that his basic retirement check would be $915.

He had an option to take smaller monthly checks and receive some of his retirement as an immediate lump-sum payment. If he chose this option, he would receive $27,000 now and $815 on a monthly basis.

Carl researched how the lump-sum payment would be taxed. Because it represented some of his own contributions and some of the government's money, only a portion of it would be taxable. However, the taxes would be at ordinary rates—neither special tax treatment nor IRA rollover was available.

Still, even after taxes, the lump sum could be invested to earn almost enough to make up for the reduced monthly check, and Carl would have some extra money, in case he needed it to make a large purchase.

Carl decided to take the lump-sum payment.

─────────────────→ ACTION ITEM ←─────────────────

Ask your tax adviser whether distributions from your before-tax savings plan will be eligible for special lump-sum rates and whether they may be rolled into an IRA. Do not assume anything!

Are government lifetime benefits the same as those from an insurance company annuity?

Government retirement plans usually resemble insurance company annuities, but your guarantee of income lies with the government, not with an insurance company. Furthermore, unlike most insurance company annuities, your monthly government retirement plan benefit can be expected to be adjusted to reflect cost-of-living changes. This adjustment is known as a COLA or cost-of-living adjustment.

→ ACTION ITEM ←

Each government retirement plan's COLA is different. Find out whether your retirement plan adjusts to meet changes in the cost of living, and when those adjustments start.

What happens to my government retirement plan if I die while still working?

Depending on how long you have been an employee, your spouse may be eligible for a one-time payout of your contributions and also a monthly annuity.

As in other retirement plans, the first $5,000 of such a benefit may be tax-free.

→ ACTION ITEM ←

Be sure *your spouse* can answer the following questions, in the event that you were to die while employed by the government:

▶ **Will I receive a one-time payment?**

▶ **How will the payment be taxed?**

▶ **Will I receive a monthly income?**

▶ **When will my monthly income begin and how long will it last?**

▶ **Will our children be eligible for any payments?**

▶ **If so, how will their payments be taxed?**

What would happen to my before-tax savings plan, if I were to die while still working?

Your before-tax savings plan money would be distributed to your beneficiaries. If your spouse is your beneficiary, he or she may roll the distribution to an IRA and postpone taxes. Any other beneficiary will have to pay taxes on the distribution. (Refer to Chapter 16 for a discussion of IRA rollovers.)

⟶ **ACTION ITEM** ⟵

Make sure the beneficiary designation is up-to-date on your government retirement plan.

Can you briefly describe the retirement system of the federal government?

The retirement system for federal employees changed in 1986. At that time, the Civil Service Retirement System (CSRS) began phasing out and the Federal Employees Retirement System (FERS) began phasing in.

These two plans are not alike. CSRS is designed for the lifetime-career government employee. It rewards long service and penalizes people who leave the system early. People covered by CSRS are not covered by social security.

FERS is more flexible. People under FERS are also covered by social security, so they build two retirement benefits side-by-side.

——————————→ ACTION ITEM ←——————————

If you are already working for the federal government, you may be covered by both CSRS and FERS. Review your choices for each program, before making any decisions to leave government employment or to withdraw your accumulated funds.

The federal government publishes excellent handbooks for your study.

If I retire from a government program not covered by social security, and then work enough years to be eligible for social security, can I receive both benefits?

You may be eligible to receive two benefits, but a special government pension offset rule may reduce your social security. Read *Social Security Factsheet No. 1*, available from any social security office, for further information on the government pension offset rule.

———————— POINTS TO REMEMBER ————————

▶ Get copies of the most recent booklets explaining your government plan.

▶ Government plans are nearly always contributory; some of your money goes into them. If you have a choice, be sure you are putting in the amount *you* believe is best for you.

▶ Voluntary, before-tax savings plans can be excellent savings vehicles. Before you contribute, find out whether deposits made to such a plan will receive special tax treatment when you withdraw the money at retirement.

▶ Government plans are often very restrictive, if you try to get money out before retirement. You may face penalties if you do get money out.

▶ Your government retirement plan may be set up to protect a surviving spouse when you die after you retire. The cost of this protection varies, depending on how much income you want your spouse to have.

▶ Most government retirement plans have a very valuable cost-of-living adjustment (COLA) built into them.

▶ Don't confuse a one-time payment from your government plan with the traditional lump-sum distribution from a corporate retirement plan.

▶ If you already receive a government pension, it is unlikely that you will also be eligible for a full social security retirement benefit.

5

Retirement Plans
That You Control

Up to this point, we have discussed only employer-sponsored retirement plans; your employer usually sets up, administers, and, with the exception of government retirement plans, contributes all or most of the money. These plans are almost always an excellent benefit, but they seldom allow you any contribution or investment choices.

You may be entitled to participate in other retirement plans that give you a wide range of contribution and investment control. With this control comes the responsibility of reviewing your family budget and learning about each of the investments, to be sure the contributions and the investments are the best for you.

If you participate in one of these retirement plans, you'll choose when to take money out, based on your personal needs and tax circumstances. Because changes take place regularly, planning for a distribution from a retirement plan is an ongoing process.

─────────────→ **ACTION ITEM** ←─────────────

Review the following list of retirement plans. Can you participate in one or more of them?

_____ **401(k) (Some sponsors give a name to this plan, such as salary reduction plan, or deferred savings plan)**

_____ **Keogh (Also called a noncorporate or self-employed plan)**

_____ **IRA**   **(Individual retirement account)**

_____ **TSA**   **(Tax-sheltered annuity; sometimes called a 403(b) plan or a 501(c)(3) plan)**

_____ **SEP**   **(Simplified employee pension)**

_____ **CODA**   **(Cash or deferred arrangement)**

_____ **ESOP**   **(Employee stock ownership plan)**

The names of some of these programs, stated as numbers and letters but no real words, make them difficult to identify and feel comfortable with. As with the other retirement plans we've talked about, they help you accumulate money toward retirement and may save current taxes as well. Don't overlook them just because they have strange-sounding names!

COMMON GOAL OF RETIREMENT PLANS

Accumulating money for retirement is the goal common to all these plans. They allow you to save money from your paycheck before taxes are taken out, and they allow the money to grow on a tax-deferred basis.

To illustrate how rewarding these programs can be, consider Table 5–1. The two middle columns show the growth of $100 per month deposited in a retirement plan earning 8 percent interest. This money is before-tax money: each month, before any taxes are taken out of a paycheck, $100 goes to a special retirement savings account. While

Table 5–1
The Accumulation Effect of $100 per Month

| Years | Accumulating and Withdrawing Money from a Retirement Plan | | No Retirement Plan |
	Before Taxes; Earning 8%	After Taxes; 28% Tax Bracket	After Taxes; 28% Bracket
5	$ 7,348	$ 5,291	$ 4,993
10	$18,295	$13,172	$11,646
20	$58,902	$42,409	$32,337

the money is in this account, the interest builds up tax-free until withdrawal. The second money column represents retirement plan money that has been withdrawn and taxed at 28 percent. The far right column illustrates the growth of the same amount ($100) deposited on an after-tax basis. First, taxes are taken out of the $100. Then, each year, the interest is taxed.

You can see that a tax-deferred retirement plan gives you a much faster way to accumulate money for your retirement.

THE MAGIC OF COMPOUNDING

Tax-deferred savings are better than after-tax savings, but the key to both is to steadily set aside $100 a month *to compound.* Imagine that the far right column of the table is your savings. During the first 10 years of depositing $100 per month, you would save $11,646 after taxes. After another 10 years, still saving $100 per month, your account would be worth $32,337! Compounding added an extra $10,000 to your account!

Regular saving early in life will remove much of the pressure of having to save later in life. If tax-deferred retirement plans are available, so much the better; your accounts, as shown in Table 5–1, will grow even faster!

TRANSLATING SAVINGS INTO INCOME

Take a final look at the power of accumulation. Compare the amount of income you can receive from your retirement accounts. By saving the same amounts as in Table 5–1, here's how your retirement income might be increased:

Income from Your Accumulated Savings

	Retirement Plan	*No Retirement Plan*
Amount of savings	$58,902	$32,337
Annual earnings at 8%	$ 4,712	$ 2,587
Monthly retirement income	$ 393	$ 216
After taxes at 28%	$ 283	$ 156

Can I get money out of these plans while I am still working?

Like corporate retirement plans, some of these retirement plans allow borrowing, and all of them allow you to withdraw money for hardship or disability (with potential penalties). We will be reviewing the ins and outs of each plan separately, in later chapters.

What do you advise about taking distributions at retirement?

Review the options for each plan separately. Follow up with greater detail about lump-sum distributions and IRA rollovers and distributions. These are covered in Chapters 14, 15, and 16.

My boss says, "We're too small to afford a retirement plan." Would any of these plans work for us?

It's certainly worth a look. Several retirement plans are designed for the small employer. Read the chapters on IRAs, Keoghs, TSAs, SEPs, and CODAs, and show them to your boss if they seem to fit. You'll have to do more than use this book to get going, but it's a start.

Because you don't have a retirement plan now doesn't mean you can't have one. Maybe the idea simply hasn't been brought up!

➔ ACTION ITEM ←

If your employer has no retirement plan, study the next six chapters, to see whether one of these retirement plans may be right for you. Don't assume somebody else has already done this research!

--- **POINTS TO REMEMBER** ---

▶ Identify the types of retirement plans available to you.
▶ Tax-deferred savings, in or out of retirement plans, build faster than savings that are taxed each year.
▶ Steady savings multiply through the magic of compounding.

6

The 401(k) Plan

*I*f you don't have a 401(k) retirement plan yet, you may soon. The 401(k) is the best liked and fastest growing of all retirement plans. Its popularity is well deserved: it is one of the few remaining tax-deferred retirement plans that gives employees control over their retirement security. If your employer offers you the chance to participate, seriously consider it. There are not many people who should not be putting money into a 401(k) plan.

WHERE 401(k) PLANS COME FROM

The name 401(k) is odd. Why doesn't it have a particular name, like IRA (individual retirement account) or Keogh (named after the Senator)? Our guess is that, by the time the legislators got to this retirement plan, they were tired of thinking up names! Whatever the reason, they named this plan after the Internal Revenue Code's Section 401 (which deals with tax-deferred savings plans of all sorts), Paragraph k (which describes this particular type of plan).

A 401(k) plan must be set up by your employer, even though a plan of this type is established solely for the benefit of the employees. Your employer must arrange with a retirement plan administrator to file the necessary paperwork with the Internal Revenue Service (IRS), the Department of Labor, and other agencies, in order to establish and administer a 401(k) retirement plan. Usually, all the costs of establishing and administering the plan are paid by your employer even though your employer receives no direct benefit.

Some employers avoid calling the plan by its generic name, 401(k). Instead, they may give their plan one of the following special names:

▶ Tax-deferred savings plan

▶ Savings plan plus

▶ Tax-deferred employee savings plan

▶ Salaried savings plan.

Your plan, however, may be called something completely different.

———————————→ ACTION ITEM ←———————

Ask your benefits representative whether your employer has a tax-deferred savings plan that is a 401(k) plan. If so, be on the lookout for legislative changes affecting the plan. Set up a file for articles and notices. Remember that the news media will refer to the 401(k) designation, not to the name your employer has chosen.

HOW THE 401(k) WORKS

Briefly, a 401(k) plan is an arrangement that lets you elect to have a percentage of your wages set aside, through payroll deduction, into a tax-deferred retirement account. The percentage may come from regular weekly or monthly paychecks or out of irregular payments such as bonuses or commissions.

Your contribution is limited to a percentage of your income, with a ceiling amount. The ceiling is $8,728 for 1992. In addition, deductions may only be taken from the first $228,860 of your annual income.

Your employer may also contribute to your 401(k) plan. Quite often, to encourage participation, employers may choose to match some or all of your contributions. For example, for every dollar you contribute to a 401(k), your employer might contribute 5 cents, 30 cents, or even another dollar! Limitations are placed on employer contributions.

If your employer offers to match your contributions, you certainly would want to put in enough to get that matching amount. Whether you are able to put in the maximum amount allowed depends on the other alternatives you have for savings.

Aside from the tax benefits you receive by contributing to a 401(k), your contributions are always 100 percent vested. Furthermore, employer contributions must be vested at least as fast as other pension plans—at most, within 7 years. (If you are working under a collective bargaining agreement, your vesting period may be as long as 10 or 11 years.) At retirement, all your employer's contributions are 100 percent vested to you.

Unfortunately, not everyone is eligible to contribute to a 401(k) plan. Generally, if your employer establishes a 401(k) plan, if you are 21, and if you work at least 1,000 hours within a 12-month period, you can participate.

CONTRIBUTION LIMITS

The employee contribution limit amount for the 401(k) was set by law in 1987. It started at $7,000, with an inflation adjustment built in each year. In 1988, the adjustment raised the contribution limit to $7,313; in 1989, to $7,627; in 1990, to $7,979; in 1991, to $8,475; and in 1992, to $8,728. In future years, it will rise again.

The 401(k) plan must follow general pension contribution rules. Your contributions to the 401(k) plan, when *added to* any matching employer contributions to the 401(k) plan (or other retirement plans you may have), cannot be greater than 25 percent of your compensation or $30,000, whichever is less.

The percentage amount allowed depends on a formula, calculated for your employer, based on the number of employees contributing and their contribution amounts. Any 401(k) plan is tested regularly by the plan administrator, to be sure higher-paid employees aren't getting a better deal than lower-paid employees.

At least once a year, a study identifies the eligible participants and compares them to the actual participants. (If you qualify to participate in a 401(k) but decide not to contribute, you are still considered a participant, for the purposes of the study.) Each year the study determines a percentage contribution limit for participants. The percentage may vary considerably: a typical range for employee contributions is anywhere from 5 percent to as high as 20 percent of income.

(The test is more complicated than this description suggests. If you need more information, contact your benefits representative or a retirement plan specialist.)

WEALTH ***Getting the Most Bang for the Buck.*** Mike and Joan
BUILDING feel they can set aside 6 percent of their income for
PROFILE retirement. Each has a 401(k) plan at work. Their question is: should each of them sign up for a 6 percent deduction, or is there a better way to do it?

Mike's plan allows him to set aside up to 12 percent of his income. The first 8 percent he saves is matched by his employer, at the rate of 50 cents on the dollar.

Joan's plan has no matching contributions, but it allows her to contribute as much as 16 percent of her income.

Mike and Joan want to get the best results from their savings. After evaluating their plans, they decide to use Mike's plan as their primary savings plan, putting in 8 percent, because of his employer's matching amount. They will also use Joan's plan, though at a lesser percentage, because it has some different investment choices that are to their advantage. When they are able to add more to long-term savings, they will add to Joan's plan.

⟶ ACTION ITEM ⟵

Ask your benefits representative what percentage contribution your 401(k) plan allows. If there is employer matching, try to contribute enough to get the full matching amount.

WHY YOUR CONTRIBUTION
SOMETIMES CHANGES

Too much money going into a plan results in adjustments, unexpected taxes, or even penalties. Therefore, all employers try their best to avoid overcontributions by their employees.

Suppose that, during the year, people drop out of the plan or, for some reason, the number of participants changes. Based on the contribution formula, the percentage that employees can contribute may change, too.

Again, these changes are in response to the very complicated and very strict rules that apply to 401(k) plans.

WEALTH   *The Best Laid Plans . . .* Bryce takes advantage of
BUILDING   all the special savings opportunities available to him.
PROFILE   For the second year, he is having 15 percent taken out
                  of his salary each month as a 401(k) contribution.

In September, Bryce gets the news that he won't be able to continue to put aside 15 percent. Rather, his contribution will have to drop to 5 percent for the rest of the year. He is disappointed, but realizes there is nothing he can do about it.

He decides to put the extra 10 percent into a regular savings account at the credit union, to keep up his good savings habits.

TAX PLANNING AROUND
A 401(k) PLAN

The reason 401(k) plans are so popular is that they offer tax benefits, both for you and your employer.

Your employer's contribution is a deductible business expense, and the money you contribute does not count as taxable income to you that year. At the end of the year, your contribution to your 401(k) plan will not show up on your W-2 form. The official term is "before-tax contribution." All the money you and your employer contribute is tax-deferred until you eventually take it out. Over time, this accumulation can amount to a very large sum of money.

As an example, if you contribute $100 per month to a 401(k) plan that is earning 8 percent interest and has no matching employer amount, your account will be worth nearly $60,000 in 20 years (see Figure 6-1). If your employer matched your contributions by adding $30 (30 percent) each month to this account, in 20 years it would be worth nearly $80,000! If you contributed $200 per month and your employer matched 10 percent, in 20 years you would have about $130,000!

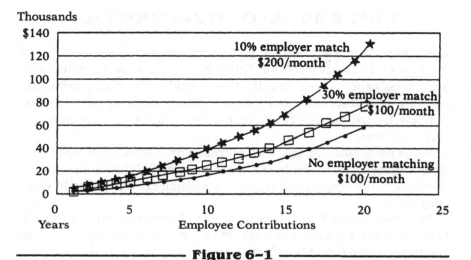

———————— Figure 6–1 ————————

Effect of changing employee contribution and employer matching.

A 401(k) plan allows you to accumulate money for your retirement very quickly.

WEALTH BUILDING PROFILE   ***The Other Shoe Drops.*** Bryce does some arithmetic when the announcement comes that he will have to reduce his 401(k) contribution from 15 to 5 percent.

He originally chose 15 percent because, with his $50,000 salary, he would be allowed to contribute $8,000 over the course of the year—the maximum allowable amount (or close to it). If his contributions drop to 5 percent for the last 4 months of the year, he'll be able to set aside only about $6,200!

When he planned for taxes, he had expected *not* to be taxed on the full $8,000 of the 401(k) contribution. Now, he has to adjust his withholding, because he faces an additional $1,800 of taxable income!

————————→ ACTION ITEM ←————————

If your percentage contribution to your 401(k) plan changes during the year, be sure to make any necessary changes in your withholding tax.

WHERE 401(k) CONTRIBUTIONS GO

Contributions to a 401(k) plan go to a trustee, who invests it according to your instructions. Your 401(k) plan almost always offers several investment choices. Usually, they include a fixed or guaranteed account, a bond account, and a stock account. These accounts may be publicly traded mutual funds or they may be private accounts directed by the trustee.

Some companies whose stock is traded on a stock exchange allow their employees to invest in the stock, as one 401(k) plan investment option. Or, the company may make matching contributions in company stock.

In any case, you decide how your contributions are to be invested. If changes are called for in your investment mix, you must take responsibility and direct the change.

WEALTH BUILDING PROFILE

Taking the Time to Manage. Sheila and Jack work for the same employer, so they have the same 401(k) choices. Every year they decide, together, how much they can afford to set aside from their paychecks.

Sheila's investment attitude is very different from Jack's. Jack chooses to put his 401(k) money into a conservative government bond fund; Sheila thinks she can make more money for herself by moving her money among the various accounts. Sometimes she invests in bonds, and at other times she moves into the stock market.

Sheila keeps up on what's happening in the economy. She regularly fills out the paperwork to shift not only her monthly contribution but also her accumulated savings from one investment category to another. She even goes so far as to have a stack of blank forms ready on her desk, for the next switch!

DECIDING WHICH INVESTMENT OPTION TO CHOOSE

A 401(k) plan investment is like any other investment. Before you pick among them, you have to know your current investment position and decide what goals your 401(k) can help you to reach. Because of the

Status While Working

Percentage-of-salary deduction, up to dollar limit ($8,728 in 1992). Employer may match.

Choice from among variety of investments.

Rollover every 12 months.

Effects of Leaving Employer

Vested over time, up to 7 years. Vested portion distributed as lump sum.

Special averaging if plan is terminated.

Pay lump-sum tax and possible penalty for early distribution, unless taken over lifetime or retiring when at least age 55.

Effects of Withdrawal While Working

Hardship withdrawal taxed; subject to early distribution penalty if under age 59 1/2.

May borrow own contributions at any age. Must repay in quarterly payments within 5 years (longer if buying a home).

After age 59 1/2, may take distribution; if not lump sum, taxed as ordinary income.

Special Circumstances

Disability

Account becomes fully vested.

Withdrawn money at any age will not be subject to early distribution penalty.

Any money withdrawn will be taxed.

Roll to an IRA or trustee-to-trustee transfer.

Lump sum eligible for special averaging.

Retirement

Account becomes fully vested.

May leave with employer, take as lump sum, roll to IRA, or do trustee-to-trustee transfer anytime. Distributions may be taxed as ordinary income, unless withdrawn as lump sum. Lump sum eligible for special tax averaging.

Distributions must start at age 70 1/2. If you are still working, you may still contribute.

Death

Account becomes fully vested and goes to beneficiary.

Beneficiary may be able to use special tax averaging.

If payout has started, beneficiary may continue.

If payout has not started, spouse may roll over to own IRA within 5 years.

Other beneficiaries must take distribution within 5 years or over life expectancy.

Taxed as ordinary income, unless lump sum. First $5,000 tax-free to beneficiary.

tax deferral associated with the 401(k), you may wish to choose investments that have the greatest potential for large gains. An example would be an investment in the stock market.

However, if investment choices within the plan are restricted or you are not able to move the money easily or quickly, it may be best to take a conservative approach to the 401(k) plan. Pick an investment that grows steadily, such as a money market fund or a fixed-income fund (an "annuity"), enjoy the tax deferral and any matching contributions, and let time and compounding work for you.

Once you participate in a 401(k) plan, you are truly an investor. Every choice you make is an investment choice, so take the time to understand what investments are available to you and how they can be expected to perform under changing economic conditions.

Review the 401(k) booklets and plan to do further outside research.

➤ ACTION ITEM ◄

Before you make investment decisions for your 401(k) plan, begin with a personal assessment. You will want to answer questions such as:

▶ **How do you feel about investing?**

▶ **How much do you know about investments and how much time will you spend keeping current on their status?**

▶ **What other investments do you have?**

▶ **How long is it until your retirement?**

Knowing the answers to these questions will help you set your 401(k) plan investment goals.

RESTRICTIONS ON INVESTING

Many 401(k) plans have restrictions on how often you can change from one investment to another. Some plans, for example, may allow switching from one investment to another only twice a year, or only at specific times during the year. Because of these restrictions, you may not be able to react quickly to changes in the economy.

There also may be administrative or paperwork delays, from the time you want to change investments until the change actually takes place. This is a significant limitation to a 401(k) plan.

SWITCHING BETWEEN INVESTMENTS

Over many years, no single investment will be the best performer. There are times when one investment will do better than others; when economic conditions change, another will do better. That's why the 401(k) usually gives you choices!

As you review your choices each year, remember to choose investments for your *current monthly* contributions *and* investments for your *accumulated* contributions. These are two different decisions, sometimes requiring two different sets of paperwork.

WEALTH   *The Time Is Right.* Max had been watching the stock
BUILDING   market move up and up for over 3 years. He had
PROFILE   watched his savings in his 401(k) plan move up, too,
                 because they were invested in a stock fund. Now, however, Max was beginning to feel uneasy. Signs had appeared that could mean the economy was in for trouble.

Max decided to move his accumulated savings from the stock fund into another choice within his plan, the money market fund. This fund wouldn't fall in value even if the economy did falter.

In 1987, Max filled out the appropriate paperwork toward the end of September. Max's request for a switch was submitted in the first week of October, but did not actually take place until the last day of the month, following regular procedures.

Unfortunately for Max, on October 19, 1987, the stock market took its biggest fall in recent decades, and Max's fortunes fell with it.

Max's good investment decision was wiped out by the delay in executing it.

GETTING MONEY OUT WHILE
STILL WORKING

Getting money out of a 401(k) plan *before* you retire is possible. The rules allow for it. However, your personal circumstances have to be

---
————————————→ ACTION ITEM ←————————————

Find out the rules governing investments in your 401(k) plan. Get answers to these questions:

▶ **What are the investment choices?**

▶ **How do I find out how well each choice is doing?**

▶ **How often can I change my investments, both for current contributions and past contributions?**

▶ **What is the time delay for the change, after I have submitted the right paperwork?**

---

just right and your administrator's policies toward taking money out will determine whether it will be possible.

Generally, before you reach age 59½, if you are still working, the only distribution allowed from a 401(k) plan is for hardship. Hardship is defined as "an immediate and heavy financial need" due to medical expenses or education costs, or because you want to purchase a principal residence. You'll have to prove that you have exhausted all other assets before you'll qualify for the hardship distribution.

Most 401(k) plans allow participants to "borrow" up to 50 percent of their vested interest, up to $50,000. Let's look at the difference between taking a distribution and borrowing.

Think of a *distribution* as a one-way trip: the money comes to you and you have no intention of putting it back. The money will be taxed, and early distribution penalties may apply.

A hardship distribution allows you to withdraw only *your* contributions, not any of the growth or interest, and none of your employer's matching amount. You may be restricted to withdrawing just enough to meet the emergency. If you are under 59½, your withdrawal may be subject to an early distribution penalty. Together, taxes and penalties could take almost half of your distribution!

Borrowing is a round trip: it implies that loan papers are drawn up, an interest rate is established, and the money will be repaid. If the loan is not fully repaid within the allotted time, the remaining amount becomes a distribution subject to taxes and possible penalties.

As with other loans from retirement plans, you need to repay the loan over no more than 5 years, with a "reasonable" interest rate (based on current rate conditions). If the loan is to help you purchase a principal residence, repayment may be spread out over more years. Payments on the loan have to be made at least quarterly.

In most cases, the interest on 401(k) loans is not deductible from your income taxes. If you are borrowing to purchase a principal residence, your interest will not be deductible unless you actually assign the home as collateral for the loan.

Furthermore, if you borrow from the plan, you will not be able to contribute to the plan for a period of time, usually one year. Because you are unable to contribute, you will lose any matching funds during this period.

If you borrow from your 401(k) plan and your loan is proper (you pay it back according to the rules), you will not be taxed and there will not be an early distribution penalty. Taxes and early distribution penalty apply to a distribution from the plan, not to a loan.

You may find it convenient to use a regular payroll deduction to pay back your loan; your employer may even require a payroll deduction. Your employer may allow you to pay off your debt more quickly by writing a check directly to the trustee or plan administrator. Find out exactly how that is done before you make plans to repay the loan that way.

WEALTH BUILDING PROFILE   *Money for College.* When Mark Hansen was in his third year of college, his college fund ran out. He needed another $7,000 to get through the school year, in addition to the money he made by working and the checks his mother Carole was able to send to him each month.

The only alternative was to borrow the money—but where? Carole could use credit card advances—and repay them at around 20 percent in interest! She could borrow through the college, as a parent, but that source was limited to $3,000, with a floating interest rate that was currently 12 percent. Carole kept looking. She discovered that she could borrow the $7,000 from her 401(k) plan, at a fixed interest rate of 10 percent.

Although it meant she wouldn't be able to participate in the plan for a year, Carole decided to borrow from the 401(k), in order to lock-in the 10 percent interest rate. With Mark's help, she would pay the loan back in less than the maximum 5-year loan period.

―――――――――――→ ACTION ITEM ◄―――――――――

If you need money, borrowing from your 401(k) plan is a reasonable idea. Before you do so, however, get answers to these questions:

▶ **How much can I borrow?**

▶ **What is the interest rate and will it change?**

▶ **What are the rules for paying the loan back?**

▶ **What penalties will I face if I borrow from my 401(k)?**

LEAVING YOUR JOB

If you leave your employment, the total vested amount of your 401(k) plan will most likely be distributed to you as a lump sum or distributed to you over a period of years. Depending on your age, you may be able to apply a special tax rate on the lump sum. Or, you may prefer to delay taxes and roll over the entire amount into an IRA. Some 401(k) plans don't require you to withdraw the money for several years. Look for the details on lump-sum distributions and IRA rollovers, in Chapters 15 and 16.

If you have a loan outstanding when you decide to leave your employer, you may be required to pay it all off, immediately.

If you are retiring, you have the same choices as someone who is leaving your employer early: take the money as a lump sum, and pay taxes at the special tax rate; have the money distributed to you over a period of years; or roll the entire amount into an IRA and delay taxes. At retirement, all of your employer contributions become fully vested. Moreover, you may be able to leave the money with the plan until you are ready or required to withdraw it.

Be sure to read about the advantages and disadvantages of leaving retirement money with the plan in Chapter 15.

Why wouldn't I put money into a 401(k) plan?

People who simply can't make ends meet wouldn't be able to commit to regular savings through a 401(k) plan. People who need to accumulate money for short-term goals (a car, or a vacation) might be able to set aside the money, but, if they placed it into a 401(k) plan, they would find it inconvenient, and probably costly, to get the money out. We can't think of any other good reasons not to participate!

If my 401(k) plan contribution doesn't show up on my W-2 form, won't my social security be affected?

No, it won't. Although the income going into the 401(k) plan doesn't count as taxable income, it does count as part of your total compensation. Your social security is based on your total compensation.

Can I get the money out of my 401(k) plan without penalty, if I am under 59½ when I retire?

Yes. If you are at least age 55 when you retire, you will avoid the early distribution penalty.

If I am younger than age 55 and receive a distribution from a 401(k) plan, can I avoid the early distribution penalty?

To avoid the early distribution penalty before age 55, you must be separated from service and either roll the entire amount into an IRA or take the distribution from your 401(k) plan as a *series of payments based on your life expectancy* (or the life expectancies of you and your spouse).

Once I am eligible to retire, can I get money out of the 401(k) plan even though I am still working?

If you take a distribution before age 59½ and you have not retired, consider borrowing from the plan, as previously discussed. Otherwise, you will have to pay an early distribution penalty along with income taxes. You should avoid this if at all possible.

If you are older than age 59½, you may take withdrawals from your 401(k) plan while you are still working, without an early distribution penalty. The withdrawals will be taxed as ordinary income, unless the entire account is distributed under the lump-sum rules.

Many employers have not yet developed the procedures to allow such withdrawals, so check whether they're available before you try this.

──────────────→ ACTION ITEM ←──────────────

**Check with your benefits representative to be
sure that withdrawals before retirement are allowed. If you anticipate making such a withdrawal,
find out the exact procedures you must follow.
Keep in mind that, if you make a withdrawal, you
will not be able to use the special lump-sum income averaging.**

───

What will happen to my 401(k) plan if I continue to work past normal retirement age?

As with other tax-deferred plans, you are required to make
a minimum withdrawal from your 401(k) at age 70½. If you
are working, this would mean that you are contributing
with one hand and taking a distribution with the other!

Determining the required minimum withdrawal is not
easy. Be in close touch with your tax adviser during the
year *before* you reach age 70½. Contact your benefits representative, to verify that the correct distribution will be
made before the required withdrawal deadline. Remember,
even if your employer is the cause of a delay or a mistake,
you will be responsible for the tax and penalties!

Should I invest in my company stock through the 401(k) plan?

If you believe that your company is a good investment and
that the stock will represent good future value, buy the
stock.

However, don't overlook the potential danger of "putting
all your eggs in one basket." If both your salary and your
retirement plan depend on the health of your company, then
you may not want to put your savings into company stock.

What happens when a distribution from my 401(k) plan is made as a result of a divorce or disability?

If a distribution is made to a nonparticipant as a result of a
qualified domestic relations order (QDRO), or to a participant as a result of total disability, there won't be an early

distribution penalty. However, unless the distribution is rolled into an IRA, it will be taxable.

Does the "success" penalty apply to 401(k) plans?

If you receive a distribution of more than $150,000 in one year ($750,000, if the distribution is made in one lump sum) from retirement plans, you may have to pay a 15 percent penalty tax on the excess. The "success" penalty is covered in more detail in Chapter 14.

→ ACTION ITEM ←

If you are receiving, from all retirement plans, more than $150,000 annually ($750,000, if the distribution is made in one lump sum), talk to your retirement plan administrator about possible ways to receive less income and avoid the 15 percent penalty tax.

What happens to my 401(k) plan if I die?

The proceeds from your 401(k) plan automatically go to your named beneficiary. If it is your spouse, he or she will have the choices you would have had if you had withdrawn the money: roll over into an IRA; take advantage of special lump-sum tax rates, if you would have been eligible for them; or take the distribution and pay ordinary income tax rates. If your beneficiary is not your spouse, that person can only receive the distribution and pay ordinary income taxes on it. However, the first $5,000 distributed from the 401(k) plan is free of taxes to the beneficiary.

There is never an early distribution penalty for a distribution made because a 401(k) plan participant died.

→ ACTION ITEM ←

Review the beneficiary designation on your 401(k) plan, to be sure that it is up-to-date.

What is different about government 401(k) plans?

Federal, state, county, and city governments, and the military, offer their employees deferred pay plans that resemble 401(k) plans. However, government plans may allow for higher contributions (as part of a catch-up provision) and for higher overall contribution limits.

In addition, government plans may have stricter rules regarding loans or distributions.

────────────→ ACTION ITEM ←────────────

If you are a government employee, check with your benefits representative regarding your tax-deferred savings plan. Use the 401(k) plan Action Items in this chapter as a guide for questions. Make note of how your government plan differs from the regular 401(k) plan rules.

──────────── **POINTS TO REMEMBER** ────────────

▸ Your contribution to a 401(k) plan is limited to a percentage of your income and has a yearly contribution ceiling ($8,728 in 1992).

▸ The percentage you are allowed to contribute depends on the number of employees at your company, how many are participating in the plan, and how much they earn. The contribution formula is recalculated regularly.

▸ Your contribution to a 401(k) plan is always 100 percent vested. Your employer's contribution may vest over a number of years.

▸ Your 401(k) plan contribution does not appear on your W-2 form, so you are not taxed on that money in the year you earned it.

▸ You must decide how the money going into your 401(k) plan is to be invested. As an investor, optimize your investment by actively managing it.

▸ You may be able to get money out of your 401(k) plan while you are still working. Taking out a loan is preferable to taking a distribution.

▶ At retirement, you have several choices regarding your 401(k) plan savings:

Take it out as a lump sum, with special lump-sum tax treatment, or

Roll it into an IRA, or

Leave it with the company and postpone the decision.

▶ If you are at least age 55 and you retire, you may take your money out of your 401(k) plan and avoid the early distribution penalty.

▶ If you die, your 401(k) plan proceeds go to your beneficiary. Spouses have different choices from other beneficiaries, regarding taxation of the money.

7

Individual Retirement Account (IRA)

*T*he IRA continues to be batted and tossed around by Congress; we regularly wonder whether it will survive. Meanwhile, we can all contribute to an IRA and many of us can deduct our contributions from our income. But does contributing to an IRA make sense any more? What do we do with the IRAs we've already established? These questions and others make IRAs one of the most complicated retirement plans we have.

Let's start with the basics.

WHAT IS AN INDIVIDUAL RETIREMENT ACCOUNT?

An individual retirement account, otherwise known as an IRA, allows you to contribute up to $2,000 each year toward your own retirement. Some, or possibly all, of this annual contribution may be tax-deductible. Your contributions are usually made to an account that offers a wide variety of investment choices, which you control.

Almost anyone receiving income from employment can contribute to an IRA. Income from employment includes wages, salaries, commissions, tips, professional fees, bonuses, and all other amounts received for providing personal services. Divorced or legally separated people receiving alimony may contribute to their own IRAs. Non-working spouses may also contribute toward their own retirement.

Keep in mind that, for IRA contribution purposes, income from employment is different from income from dividends, interest, capital gains, retirement plan contributions, or deferred compensation. You cannot contribute to an IRA if you only receive these types of nonemployment income. If you also receive income from employment, you must combine it with your nonemployment income to determine whether your IRA contributions are tax-deductible.

RULES REGARDING THE TAX-DEDUCTIBILITY OF IRA CONTRIBUTIONS

Rules regarding the tax-deductibility of IRA contributions seem to change every few years. In 1992, if two specific tests are met, you can deduct the lesser of $2,000 or 100 percent of your employment income.

At present, you may deduct contributions to an IRA if:

▸ Neither you nor your spouse is a "covered participant" for any part of the year in a retirement plan, or

▸ You are a "covered participant" in a retirement plan, and your adjusted gross income (AGI) is less than the "income limit."

FIRST DEDUCTIBILITY TEST: "COVERED PARTICIPANT"

The first test in determining the tax-deductibility of your IRA contributions is to know whether *either* you or your spouse is a "covered participant" in a retirement plan for *any* part of the year. A covered participant is someone eligible (accruing a benefit) under a pension, profit-sharing, ESOP, TSA, Keogh, 401(k), SEP, CODA, or government-sponsored retirement plan.

If your (or your spouse's) employer has any of these retirement plans, you will probably be considered a covered participant even though you may not have contributed to the plan in a particular year. There is one exception to this rule: under defined-contribution plans, you are not a covered participant if annual contributions are not made to the plan.

Usually, the W-2 Form you receive each year from your employer indicates whether you are a covered participant. If it doesn't, you must check with your employer to see whether you are covered. Don't forget to check with your spouse's employer too!

INDIVIDUAL RETIREMENT ACCOUNT (IRA) OVERVIEW

Status While Working

Contributions up to $2,000 per year; $2,250, if spousal.
May be deductible, depending on income level and other retirement benefits.
Choices available among variety of investments.
Rollover every 12 months; trustee-to-trustee transfer, anytime.

Effects of Leaving Employer

100% vested at all times.
Rollover to another IRA once every 12 months; trustee-to-trustee transfer, anytime.
May no longer contribute, unless receiving income from employment.
Withdrawals before age 59$^{1/2}$ subject to early distribution penalty, unless taken over lifetime.

Effects of Withdrawal While Working

May not borrow from account.
Any money withdrawn will be taxed.
Money withdrawn prior to age 59$^{1/2}$ subject to early distribution penalty, unless received over life expectancy.

Special Circumstances

Disability

Withdrawn money, at any age, not subject to early distribution penalty.
Any money withdrawn will be taxed.
Rollover every 12 months; trustee-to-trustee transfer, anytime.

Retirement

All distributions taxed as ordinary income.
Must begin distributions by age 70$^{1/2}$.
Distributions prior to age 59$^{1/2}$ subject to early distribution penalty, unless taken over lifetime.
Not eligible for 10-year or 5-year special averaging.
Rollover every 12 months; trustee-to-trustee transfer, anytime.

Death

Account goes to beneficiary.
If payout has started, beneficiary must continue payout.
If payout has not started, spouse may roll over to another IRA within 5 years.
Other beneficiaries must take distribution within 5 years or over life expectancy.
All distributions taxed as ordinary income. First $5,000 tax-free to beneficiary.
Early distribution penalty not applicable to beneficiaries.

WEALTH   *When It Pays to Remember.* Marian, just out of engi-
BUILDING   neering school, landed a good job with a jet engine
PROFILE   manufacturer. Her starting pay was $38,000, much
                  higher than the average, but she had graduated from
a top school with top honors.

The company has a retirement program, but all employees are
required to be with the company for 1 year before they can contribute
to the plan.

Marian seemed to recall having heard that, if an employer was not
contributing to a retirement plan, the employees could contribute to
an IRA and deduct it. She thought that, because there was a 1-year
wait before contributions began in her plan, she should be able to
contribute to an IRA and deduct the full amount.

When she met with her tax preparer, she found that she had re-
membered this information correctly. Because a 1-year wait is a requirement under her retirement plan, she is not considered covered
during this period. The IRA is something she can contribute to (and
deduct) during her first year.

Remember, you can deduct an IRA only if neither you nor your spouse
is a participant in a retirement plan. If *either* of you is a participant,
then IRA tax-deductibility depends on the IRA "income-limit" test.

─────────────→ **ACTION ITEM** ←─────────────
**Find out from your employer whether you are a cov-
ered participant in a retirement plan. Check with
your spouse's employer, too.**

SECOND DEDUCTIBILITY TEST:
"INCOME LIMIT"

The second test to determine the tax-deductibility of your IRA contributions involves knowing your adjusted gross income (AGI), usually
the amount shown on the last line of the front page of your Form 1040
tax return. Your AGI includes income from interest, dividends, capital

gains, the taxable portion of your social security, and your retirement or employment income.

The test modifies the AGI slightly by calculating it without any deduction for an IRA or for any foreign income or foreign housing.

If either you or your spouse is a covered participant of a retirement plan, each of you may deduct some portion of your IRA contributions, as long as your AGI does not go over a certain amount. The portion you can deduct will vary, depending on whether you are single, or are married and filing separate or joint tax returns.

Tables 7–1 and 7–2 will help you determine whether you can deduct all or a portion of your IRA contribution.

WEALTH BUILDING PROFILE   *Contribution But No Deduction.* Millie and Sam are employed. Millie earns $30,000 as a lab technician for a local pharmacy. The pharmacy does not have a retirement plan for its employees. Sam, who works for a large automobile manufacturer, earns $35,000. The automobile

Table 7–1
How Much You Can Deduct

Adjusted Gross Income (AGI)			
Single Person or Head of Household	Married Couple Filing Jointly or Qualifying Widow	Married Couple Filing Separately	Allowable Deduction
$35,000 or greater	$50,000 or greater	$10,000 or greater	$ 0
34,000	49,000	9,000	200
33,000	48,000	8,000	400
32,000	47,000	7,000	600
31,000	46,000	6,000	800
30,000	45,000	5,000	1,000
29,000	44,000	4,000	1,200
28,000	43,000	3,000	1,400
27,000	42,000	2,000	1,600
26,000	41,000	1,000*	1,800
25,000 or less	40,000 or less	$ 1*	2,000

* Limited to 100 percent of earnings.

Note: For income between amounts shown, IRA deductions are prorated.

Table 7-2

Internal Revenue Service Information Chart on IRA Deductions (from IRS Publication 590)

CAN YOU TAKE AN IRA DEDUCTION?

If Your Modified AGI* is:		If You Are Covered by a Retirement Plan at Work and Your Filing Status is:				If You Are Not Covered by a Retirement Plan at Work and Your Filing Status is:		
		• Single • Head of Household	• Married Filing Jointly (even if your spouse is not covered by a plan at work) • Qualifying Widow(er)	Married Filing Separately**	Married Filing Jointly (and your spouse is covered by a plan at work)	• Single • Head of Household	• Married Filing Jointly or Separately (and your spouse is not covered by a plan at work) • Qualifying Widow(er)	Married Filing Separately (even if your spouse is covered by a plan at work)***
At Least	But Less Than	You Can Take	You Can Take	You Can Take	You Can Take	You Can Take	You Can Take	You Can Take
$-0-	$10,000	Full deduction	Full deduction	Partial deduction	Full deduction	Full Deduction	Full Deduction	Full Deduction
$10,000	$25,000	Full deduction	Full deduction	No deduction	Full deduction			
$25,000	$35,000	Partial deduction	Full deduction	No deduction	Full deduction			
$35,000	$40,000	No deduction	Full deduction	No deduction	Full deduction			
$40,000	$50,000	No deduction	Partial deduction	No deduction	Partial deduction			
$50,000 or over		No deduction	No deduction	No deduction	No deduction			

*Modified AGI (adjusted gross income) is: (1) for Form 1040A—the amount on line 14 increased by any excluded series EE bond interest shown on Form 8815, Exclusion of Interest from Series EE U.S. Savings Bonds Issued after 1989, or (2) for Form 1040—the amount on line 31, figured without taking into account any IRA deduction or any foreign earned income exclusion and foreign housing exclusion (deduction), or any series EE bond interest exclusion from Form 8815.

**If you did not live with your spouse at any time during the year, your filing status is considered, for this purpose, as Single (therefore your IRA deduction is determined under the "Single" column).

***You are entitled to the full deduction only if you did not live with your spouse at any time during the year. If you did live with your spouse during the year, you are, for this purpose, treated as though you are covered by a retirement plan at work (therefore, your IRA deduction is determined under the "Married Filing Separately" column in the "If You Are Covered by a Retirement Plan..." section of the chart).

manufacturer has a mandatory retirement plan for all its employees. Sam has no way of excluding himself from it.

Millie and Sam's adjusted gross income is over the $50,000 income limit for married couples filing a joint return.

Because Sam is eligible for a retirement plan and their income exceeds the income limit, they can contribute to IRAs, but cannot deduct them.

If your adjusted gross income is less than the income limit, then some portion of your IRA contributions can be deducted. This deduction would be allowed even if one of you is a covered participant in a retirement plan.

WEALTH   *How Much to Deduct.* Tom and Janice file a joint tax
BUILDING   return. They both work, and Tom has a retirement
PROFILE   plan through his employer. Their adjusted gross in-
come (AGI) is $46,000: $30,000 from Tom's salary, and $16,000 from Janice's salary. They want to contribute only the deductible amount to an IRA, but are not sure how much is deductible.

Using the information in Tables 7–1 and 7–2, they find that, with a combined $46,000 AGI on a joint return, the maximum deductible contribution is $800.

━━━━━━━━→ ACTION ITEM ←━━━━━━━━

Don't overlook a possible IRA deduction. Check each year to see whether your AGI is above or below the allowable income limit.

SPOUSAL IRAs

Special IRA rules exist for nonworking spouses and for spouses earning less than $250 per year. Generally, if you file a joint tax return, a nonworking spouse or a spouse with annual earnings of $250 or less can contribute to a spousal IRA. The working spouse can contribute to a regular IRA.

The maximum annual combined contribution to both a regular and a spousal IRA is $2,250. You may divide up the contribution any way you like, but no more than $2,000 can go into one account.

A spousal IRA is a completely separate IRA account held solely in the spouse's name. Your own regular IRA is held in your name alone. Each account is an *individual* retirement account.

Contributing to a spousal IRA and then deducting that IRA contribution is another matter. Your right to deduct the IRA contribution will depend on whether either of you is a covered participant in an employer-sponsored retirement plan and whether you pass the income-limit test.

The rule is: If spouses file jointly and either spouse is ineligible to deduct an IRA, then both spouses are ineligible.

MAXIMIZING SPOUSAL IRAs

From a retirement planning standpoint, if one spouse is older, there could be an advantage to contributing the maximum amount to the younger spouse's IRA. This advantage occurs when the older spouse reaches age 70$\frac{1}{2}$ and begins mandatory withdrawals. If the added income is not needed, the older spouse would have a much smaller IRA and, therefore, smaller withdrawals. The larger IRA continues to grow, undisturbed.

This works the other way, too. You may need to receive as much income as you can, early in your retirement. In this case, make maximum contributions to the older spouse's IRA. At age 59$\frac{1}{2}$, the older spouse can receive maximum income without penalty and without having to wait for the younger spouse to reach withdrawal age.

**WEALTH
BUILDING
PROFILE**

Thinking Ahead. By age 65, Fernando began to feel tired of working and longed for more freedom. Both he and his wife, Esther, decided that now would be a good time to sell their business and live off the proceeds.

When the business was sold 6 months later, they were surprised at the amount of money it brought in. Their proceeds almost equaled

Fernando's income while they had operated the business! Based
on the terms of the sale, the income would last for 10 years, until
Fernando was 75.

During their working years, they had contributed $2,250 annually
to IRAs. Fernando, being older than Esther, put only $250 into his
IRA; Esther put $2,000 into her nonworking spousal IRA. They had
reasoned that they would not need income from IRAs for many
years, and they wanted to delay withdrawal as long as possible.

When Fernando reached age 70½, he was required to begin withdrawing money from his IRA. Because of their long-term planning,
however, his account value was only a fraction of Esther's. Had he
contributed the $2,000 annually to his IRA instead of Esther's, the
income from the IRA and the resulting taxes would have been much
more.

When the income from the sale of the business ended, Esther's
larger IRA withdrawals helped to even out their income.

──────────────→ ACTION ITEM ◆──────────────
**If you are contributing to a regular IRA and a
spousal IRA, review the amounts you are contributing to each account. Determine whether it would be
better to contribute more to one account than to
the other.**

NONDEDUCTIBLE IRAs

You can continue to contribute to an IRA even though you cannot
deduct your contribution for tax purposes. If you have made a nondeductible contribution to your IRA, the earnings (interest, dividends,
and capital gains) are tax-deferred until withdrawn.

Whether you *should* contribute to a nondeductible IRA is another
matter. It is always a good idea to save money regularly, particularly
if you can save money tax-deferred. Why then would you *not* want to
use nondeductible IRAs? The primary disadvantage is that, under
current regulations, once you start making nondeductible IRA contributions, you are required to fill out and file Form 8606 with the

federal government each year. When you want to take money out of your nondeductible IRA, there are withdrawal restrictions. (Chapter 14 discusses these problems.) These regulations often make a nondeductible IRA more trouble than it is worth.

Many tax-deferred investments are readily available as alternatives to nondeductible IRAs. The most common alternatives are single-premium deferred annuities, municipal bonds, and U.S. government savings bonds. All of these investments allow your earnings to be tax-free or tax-deferred. Furthermore, you are not restricted to a maximum of $2,000 in any of these investments.

→ **ACTION ITEM** ←

If you are contributing to a nondeductible IRA, research alternative tax-deferred investments that don't require extra reporting and have no limits on investment amounts.

If you made a contribution during the year and find out before year-end that the contribution is not deductible, you may leave it in the IRA and treat it as a nondeductible IRA. If, however, you do not want to contribute to a nondeductible IRA, a withdrawal must be made by the due date of the return (including extensions), to avoid an early distribution penalty.

WEALTH BUILDING PROFILE *The Penalties Mount.* Marie is eligible for a retirement plan. Her maximum deductible contribution, based on her $31,000 AGI, is $800. If Marie claimed a full $2,000 IRA deduction on her income tax return and did not correct it by the due date of the return (plus extensions), she would have to file an amended return showing the excess IRA deduction. A 10 percent early distribution penalty would be charged on $1,200 ($2,000 minus $800), even though she left the money in the IRA! She would pay $120 in penalties.

MAKING IRA CONTRIBUTIONS

You can contribute to your IRA at any time during the year. However, contributions can be delayed until you file your income tax return, but no later than April 15 (depending on weekends), even if you file for an extension. Contributing early in the year allows your money to compound over a longer period of time.

Table 7-3 compares an annual $2,000 IRA contribution made at the beginning of the year with the same contribution made at the end of the year. Each account earns 6 percent interest.

WEALTH
BUILDING
PROFILE

Understanding the Magic of Compounding. Bob and Pat contributed $2,250 each year to their IRA and spousal IRA. From his early days in the banking business, Bob remembered that compounding interest was most rewarding when given time. Bob and Pat were determined to earn everything they could on their IRAs. Each year, on the very first banking day, they deposited their annual contribution.

Over the years, they averaged 8 percent interest on their money. After 25 years, the accounts were worth $177,647. This is substantially more than the $164,488 that the accounts would have been worth if they had made their contributions at the end of each year.

Bob and Pat took advantage of the magic of compounding.

Table 7-3
Making Early IRA Contributions

Year	Contribution Made on Jan. 1 of Each Year (End-of-Year Values)	Contribution Made on Dec. 31 of Each Year (End-of-Year Values)
1	$ 2,120	$ 2,000
2	4,367	4,120
3	6,749	6,367
4	9,274	8,749
5	11,950	11,274
10	27,943	26,362
20	77,985	73,571

One of the major advantages of the IRA is its contribution flexibility. The maximum contribution to your own IRA is $2,000. You choose, each year, the amount (up to $2,000) that you would like to contribute.

→ ACTION ITEM ←

If you are contributing regularly to IRAs, take advantage of the power of compounding by making your contribution as early in the year as possible.

OVERCONTRIBUTIONS

If you contribute more than the rules allow, you have made an overcontribution. Overcontributions to an IRA may be subject to a 6 percent excise tax, unless you withdraw the money before the due date of the tax return (including extensions). Additionally, all *earnings* on this excess contribution may be subject to an early distribution penalty.

If you made an overcontribution to this year's IRA, you can apply it to next year's IRA contribution, if the overcontribution is less than next year's regular IRA contribution.

WEALTH BUILDING PROFILE   *Allocating an Overcontribution.* In 1991, Tracy contributed $1,400 to her IRA. Based on her AGI, she was allowed to deduct only $1,000. Because she did not withdraw the excess by the due date of the return, she had an overcontribution of $400. Tracy is faced with paying a penalty or applying this overcontribution to her 1992 IRA.

In 1992, Tracy's deductible IRA contribution, based on her AGI, is $1,500. To avoid paying a penalty on her 1991 cvercontribution, Tracy contributes $1,100 to her 1992 IRA and deducts $1,500 ($1,100 from 1992 plus $400 from 1991).

BORROWING AND WITHDRAWING

Unlike most other retirement plans, IRAs don't permit borrowing, with one minor exception. Generally, you will be taxed if you withdraw money for any reason. If money is withdrawn prior to age 59½, an early distribution penalty may also apply.

The exception has to do with IRA rollover rules. These rules, if followed correctly, allow you to withdraw your IRA for 60 days and move it to another IRA, once in every 12-month period. By using the IRA rollover rules, you haven't borrowed the money but you still have the use of the money for up to 60 days with no penalty. Some people consider this a way of getting around the borrowing rules, even if they can have the money for only 60 days.

When you want to withdraw money from your IRA, you can avoid the early distribution penalty *at any age* if you elect an annuity, which is a payout spread over your entire life expectancy or over the joint life expectancy of you and your beneficiary. Alternately, you can avoid the penalty by electing a payout spread over at least 5 years or until you reach age 59½, whichever term is longer. After that, if you did not elect an irrevocable payout option, you can increase, lower, or even stop your withdrawals.

For *all* retirement plans, if you become permanently and totally disabled, or die, you or your beneficiaries will *not* be subject to the early distribution penalty.

WEALTH BUILDING PROFILE   *Tapping a Retirement Account.* Kent took early retirement at age 55 and bought the franchise for a computerized print shop. The purchase took a lot of his built-up savings, and, for the first few years, he doesn't expect much personal income from the new business.

Kent needs extra income and has thought about tapping his IRA account, but he is put off by the stiff early distribution penalty.

He is excited to learn that he *can* begin withdrawals from his IRA, without a penalty, by using a new option made available in the 1986 tax law revisions.

The option works this way: as long as Kent takes a "scheduled series of substantially equal payments for his lifetime," he'll pay only income taxes, with no penalty.

Kent asks his financial planner to help him calculate the exact amount of the payment, because he isn't sure how to make the life expectancy and interest rate assumptions that are required. Together, they discover that Kent can receive a distribution of around $4,000 a year from the IRA. (Kent's IRA has approximately $50,000 on deposit.)

Even more interesting, as long as Kent continues to receive payments for 5 years, he can then reassess his situation. If the print shop is successful, he can reduce the IRA withdrawals or interrupt them altogether! The "lifetime" withdrawal method fits Kent's circumstances perfectly.

A final note on borrowing. Using your IRA as collateral is a form of borrowing. If you use it as collateral for a loan, the value of the account will be taxed as a distribution.

INVESTING IN AN IRA

To invest in an IRA, you will need to contact a bank, savings and loan, credit union, insurance company, stock brokerage firm, mutual fund, or trust company specializing in IRAs. You may prefer to open your account in person, but you can do it by mail, too. Remember that the IRS registers the date the account opens, not the postmark date of your mailed deposit.

If you lose money in your IRA investment, you must first determine whether the losses are from a deductible IRA or a nondeductible IRA. Deductible IRAs do not allow you to take losses. Nondeductible IRAs, however, allow you to deduct losses, if your distributions are less than your contributions plus earnings.

WEALTH BUILDING PROFILE   *Deducting Losses.* Victor invested in nondeductible IRAs. In 1990, he put $2,000 into a CD; in 1991, he invested $2,000 in stocks. He retired in 1992 and decided to withdraw his IRA money.

From 1990 to 1992, his CD earned $400 of interest, for a total ending value of $2,400. His IRA stock account, however, lost $500, for a total ending value of $1,500.

The combined total of both accounts at the time of withdrawal was $3,900 ($2,400 plus $1,500) or $100 less than his contributions. Victor claimed a $100 loss on his income taxes for 1992.

MOVING FROM ONE IRA
TO ANOTHER

You are allowed to roll over (move) each of your current IRAs to another IRA *once every 12 months*, not once each calendar year. If you roll over any portion of an IRA more frequently, you will be taxed as though you have received a distribution.

If you prefer, ask your IRA trustee to transfer the account directly to another trustee, without your receiving the money. This trustee-to-trustee transfer may be done as often as you like.

To avoid getting trapped, use an IRA trustee with many investment options. IRA rollovers and trustee-to-trustee transfers are discussed in greater detail in Chapter 16.

→ **ACTION ITEM** ←

Ask your current IRA trustee for a list of investment options available in your IRA. Determine whether these investment options are suitable for your goals. If not, find a bank, savings and loan, credit union, insurance company, stock brokerage firm, mutual fund, or trust company specializing in IRAs, that will allow the investment options you want for your IRA.

If I am contributing to another retirement plan, can I deduct my IRA contribution?

If either you or your spouse is contributing to a 401(k), Keogh, TSA, or any other retirement plan, and your AGI is greater than the IRA deductibility income test, your IRA contributions cannot be deducted. If, however, *neither* you nor your spouse is contributing to a retirement plan, you did not contribute to one at any time during the year, and no employer contributions are being made, your IRA contributions can be deducted.

What happens to the spousal IRA if my spouse earns more than $250?

Your spouse can earn up to $250 annually and still make a spousal IRA contribution. If your spouse earns more than $250, set up a separate regular IRA. Your spouse can then contribute 100 percent of his or her earnings up to $2,000.

If I am still working at age 70^1/$_2$, am I eligible to contribute to an IRA?

If you are 70^1/$_2$ by the end of the tax year, you cannot make further contributions to your IRA, even though you may still be working.

If I am still working at age 70^1/$_2$, may I contribute to a nonworking spousal IRA?

If the nonworking spouse is younger than age 70^1/$_2$ at the end of the tax year, a spousal IRA is allowed.

If my spouse and I are separated, can I take a deduction for my IRA?

If you are married, filing a separate return, and not covered by a retirement plan, but your spouse is covered, you can take an IRA deduction if you did not live together at any time during the tax year. If you are covered by a retirement plan, the income-limit test applies.

May a divorced or separated individual contribute to an IRA, if income is limited to alimony?

Taxable alimony or separate maintenance payment is income and is qualified for IRA contributions. The divorced or separated individual must not have employment income and the IRA must have been set up before the divorce or separation. If you are receiving taxable alimony or separate maintenance, you can contribute 100 percent of this income, up to $2,000, to your own IRA.

May one divorced spouse transfer IRA assets to the other divorced spouse?

One divorced spouse may transfer IRA assets to the former spouse if the transfer is made under a valid court decree known as a qualified domestic relations order (QDRO).

───────────── ➤ **ACTION ITEM** ◄ ─────────────

If you are planning to divorce, review your IRA plans *before* you sign the final papers. You may wish to set up an IRA based on alimony or separate maintenance, or have IRA assets transferred tax-free under a qualified domestic relations order.

Can my employer contribute to my IRA?

Yes. This is generally referred to as a simplified employee pension plan (SEP or SEP-IRA). Your employer could contribute the lesser of 15 percent of your income or $30,000. Furthermore, if you make contributions to your SEP-IRA, you can deduct them in the same way that you deduct contributions to a regular IRA, that is, the lesser of 100 percent of your compensation or $2,000 ($2,250 for a spousal IRA). SEPs are discussed in greater detail in Chapter 11.

───────────── **POINTS TO REMEMBER** ─────────────

▸ At present, you may contribute to an IRA if you have employment income and are under age 70½.
▸ You may deduct an IRA if neither you or your spouse has a retirement plan or your adjusted gross income is less than a certain limit.
▸ Nonworking spouses and divorced spouses follow special rules for contributing to and deducting IRAs.

▶ Under current regulations, saving money using a nondeductible IRA may be more trouble than it is worth.

▶ Unlike most other retirement plans, IRAs don't permit borrowing.

▶ You may begin withdrawals from your IRA before age 59½, without penalty, by taking a "lifetime payout."

▶ You may be able to deduct losses incurred in nondeductible IRAs.

▶ You can use the rollover privilege to give yourself different investment options for your IRA.

8

Tax-Sheltered
Annuity (TSA)

A tax-sheltered annuity, commonly called a TSA, is a special retirement savings plan for employees of public schools and certain tax-exempt organizations. A TSA is considered to be the most generous and flexible of any retirement plan, but the rules allow only a particular group of employees to take advantage of it.

This chapter explores the eligibility requirements and benefits of a TSA. If you qualify, you should take advantage of this retirement plan.

QUALIFYING FOR A TSA

To qualify for TSA contributions, you must be employed by an educational institution or by a tax-exempt organization operated exclusively for religious, charitable, scientific, public-safety testing, literary, or educational purposes. Organizations for the prevention of cruelty to children or animals or for the fostering of national or international sports competition also qualify.

Sometimes, these tax-exempt employers are called "501(c)(3) organizations," after the Internal Revenue Code section that covers charitable employers. A corporation, community chest, fund, or foundation may qualify. Public schools and churches, the most common qualified employers, are usually called 403(b) organizations.

Qualifying employees must be employed either full-time or part-time. Independent contractors to these organizations may not contribute to a TSA.

TSAs AND OTHER
RETIREMENT PLANS

Contributions to a TSA, made by either you or your employer, must be invested in either an annuity contract from a life insurance company or in mutual fund shares purchased through a custodial account. Church employees may also contribute to a special kind of church-maintained defined-contribution plan called an "income account." If you are making contributions to a TSA, all of your contributions must be made through payroll deductions.

Although your organization may qualify for contribution to TSAs, it is not limited to using only a TSA. You may just as easily have a 401(k) plan or a simplified employee pension (SEP).

Of all retirement plans, TSAs are considered to be the best; you can generally save more of your income in this type of retirement plan than in any other.

→ **ACTION ITEM** ←

Check with your benefits department to deter-mine whether your employer is a qualified organi-zation for TSA purposes.

CONTRIBUTING TO A TSA

Your amount of TSA contributions will vary, depending on whether you and/or your employer are contributing to the TSA or whether you are participating in certain retirement plans other than your TSA.

Generally, if you make all the contributions to your TSA (with no employer contributions), the maximum annual contribution allowed is 16% of your income up to $9,500. If your employer contributes to your TSA, the maximum combined contribution cannot exceed the lesser of 25 percent of your income or $30,000. With employer contri-butions, your own contributions can still not exceed $9,500. Your contributions must be made entirely through payroll deductions.

The contribution maximum amount of $9,500 may vary in some cases, depending on the "exclusion allowance." This complex formula is based on years of service, past contributions, and current income.

TAX-SHELTERED ANNUITY (TSA) OVERVIEW

Status While Working

Employee contributes up to 16% of salary up to $9,500 limit.

Employer contributions may be up to 25% of income or $30,000.

Employee may contribute more than $9,500 under "exclusion allowance."

Choices available are annuity contracts or mutual funds.

May move between annuity contracts anytime.

Effects of Leaving Employer

100% vested at all times.

May no longer contribute unless working for another qualified employer.

May borrow up to half account value. (See Effects of Withdrawal While Working.)

Roll over at least half of account value to IRA or trustee-to-trustee transfer anytime.

Withdrawals before age 59½ subject to early distribution penalty unless taken over lifetime.

Money withdrawn (not borrowed) at any age taxed as ordinary income. (See Effects of Withdrawal While Working.)

Effects of Withdrawal While Working

May borrow up to half account value. Borrowed funds must be repaid in quarterly payments, in 5 years (longer if purchasing a home).

Interest is not deductible.

Money withdrawn (not borrowed) prior to age 59½ subject to early distribution penalty, unless received over life expectancy.

Money withdrawn (not borrowed) at any age taxed as ordinary income.

Special Circumstances

Disability

Distributions at any age not subject to early distribution penalty.

Distributions taxed.

May borrow up to half of account value. (See Effects of Withdrawal While Working.)

Contributions stop.

Roll over at least half of account value to IRA or trustee-to-trustee transfer anytime.

Retirement

All distributions (not borrowed) taxed as ordinary income.

Distribution before age 59½ subject to early distribution penalty, unless taken over lifetime.

May borrow up to half of account value. (See Effects of Withdrawal While Working.)

Must begin distribution by age 70½.

Not eligible for 10-year or 5-year special averaging.

Roll over at least half of account value to IRA or trustee-to-trustee transfer anytime.

Death
> Account goes to beneficiary.
> If payout has started, beneficiary must continue payout.
> If payout has not started, spouse may roll over to IRA within 5 years.
> Other beneficiaries must take distribution within 5 years or over life expectancy.
> All distributions taxed as ordinary income. First $5,000 tax-free to beneficiary.
> Early distribution penalty not applicable to beneficiaries.

Because the formula is so complicated, you'll want to ask a TSA specialist to help you figure it out. If you would rather do it yourself, request a (free) copy of Publication 571 from your regional office of the Internal Revenue Service.

Some TSA-qualified employers have established a 401(k) plan or a SEP for their employees, in addition to TSAs. If this is your situation, the maximum combined contribution to these retirement plans is the greater of $9,500 or your exclusion allowance.

If you have more than a 50 percent control in a corporate retirement plan or Keogh, you must calculate these contributions along with the TSA, to determine your maximum TSA contribution. Contributions to these retirement plans reduce TSA contribution amounts dollar for dollar.

→ **ACTION ITEM** ←

Contact your benefits department and find out the names of representatives from some of the popular TSAs offered through your employer. Meet with them and determine your allowable TSA contribution.

Once a contribution amount is established and payroll deduction has begun, it can only be changed once per calendar year. However, you can stop your contribution any time.

WEALTH   *First-Year Teacher.* Gwen begins her new teaching
BUILDING   assignment in September. Because she is eager to set
PROFILE   aside the maximum amount possible into her TSA, she
                    meets with the TSA representative well before she re-
ceives her first paycheck.

They determine that her maximum contribution is 16 percent of her
$25,000 salary, or $4,000 per year. This means a deduction of $400
every month. (Gwen's school district pays during 10 months each year,
not 12 months.)

At first, Gwen expected to be able to put aside only $1,200 for her
first year: $400 each for October, November, and December. However,
she discovers that, by taking advantage of the "one-change-per-year"
rule for the last 3 months of the year, she can increase her contribution
amount.

She carefully fills out the paperwork requesting that $1,250 (50
percent of her monthly pay) be taken out of her paycheck each month!
By the end of the year, she will have been able to set aside 3 × $1,250, or
$3,750, which is within her maximum contribution limit.

In January, she will submit a second set of instructions, to restore
her paycheck reduction to 16 percent per month for the full year.

Gwen takes full advantage of the tax savings available through the
TSA. Now all she has to do is manage her budget to live on the greatly
reduced first year's paycheck!

If you contribute too much to your TSA, your excess contribution is
not deductible. You must take it out by April 15. If you withdraw it
later, it will be taxed and possibly penalized.

MOVING FROM ONE TSA
TO ANOTHER

It is quite likely that, at some point, you may want to move your TSA to
another TSA. The easiest way to accomplish this is to let the trustees
of your old and new TSAs handle the transfer for you. If you decide to
move the money yourself, you will receive a check from your old TSA.
You must then move this money into another TSA within 60 days, to

avoid taxes and possible penalties. (The same rules apply to IRA rollovers.)

Unlike an IRA, which is restricted to a rollover once every 12 months, your TSA may be moved as often as you like.

BORROWING FROM YOUR TSA

Borrowing from TSAs is allowed; you may borrow up to half of a TSA's value. Borrowing from a TSA follows the same general rules as borrowing from corporate retirement plans: you must repay the loan in regular quarterly payments, within 5 years. The repayment period may be longer, if you are purchasing a home with the borrowed money.

Keep in mind that interest paid on loans from TSAs is not deductible.

How can I contribute to my TSA early in the year and get the maximum benefit of compounding?

The earlier in the year you contribute to any retirement plan, the larger your retirement benefit will be. IRAs and Keoghs work well with this method, because contributions can be made on January 1. TSA contributions have to be made via payroll deduction, so your contribution will be spread over the year. By spreading contributions over the entire year, the effect of compounding is reduced but not totally lost.

As an example, if you invested $1,200 in an IRA at the beginning of each year and your account earned a steady 8 percent, at the end of 10 years the account would be worth $18,774. Using a TSA, and investing $100 at the end of each month, with the same earnings figure and over the same period of time, your annual $1,200 would be worth $18,294—some $500 less than the IRA.

What happens to my TSA if I leave my employer?

If you leave your employer, your account becomes frozen. No new contributions can be made, unless you work for another TSA-qualified employer. Your TSA can remain frozen as long as you like or you can roll it over into an IRA.

After I retire, am I eligible to withdraw my TSA in one lump sum and use special averaging?

No. Special tax averaging methods do not apply to lump-sum distributions from TSAs. However, a distribution of at least 50 percent of your TSA account is eligible for an IRA rollover.

Are distributions from my tax-sheltered annuity always treated as ordinary income?

Any amount not rolled over into an IRA will be treated as ordinary income when distributed to you. Furthermore, if a distribution is made to you before age 59^1/$_2$ and not rolled over into an IRA, an early distribution penalty may apply.

Are there any distributions from a TSA that can't be rolled over?

If you receive a TSA distribution as a series of payments, often called an annuity, the money may not be rolled over into an IRA. A distribution of less than half the value of the account also can't be rolled into an IRA.

What is the advantage of an IRA rollover?

An IRA rollover is one of two ways for you to postpone taxes due on a distribution from a TSA. The other way is to leave the money as a TSA.

Will I always be penalized, if I withdraw money from my TSA prior to age 59^1/$_2$?

Prior to age 59^1/$_2$, the early distribution penalty does not apply to distributions paid as follows:

▸ To your beneficiary in the event of your death
▸ To you because you are totally and permanently disabled
▸ To you at any age, in equal payments over your life expectancy, if you have separated from service
▸ To you after you have reached age 55 *and* become separated from service

▶ To you because you have deductible medical care
▶ To the person designated under a qualified domestic relations order (QDRO).

───────────────▶ ACTION ITEM ◀───────────────

If you are younger than age 59¹/₂ and you withdraw money from your TSA, use the special distribution rules (shown immediately above) to determine whether an early distribution penalty applies.

───

If I am contributing to a TSA, can I deduct a contribution to an IRA?

If you are contributing to a TSA and your AGI is greater than the IRA income-limit test as discussed in Chapter 7, you cannot deduct your IRA.

Does the success penalty apply to TSAs?

If you receive an annual distribution of more than $150,000 ($750,000, if the distribution is a lump sum) from retirement plans, you may have to pay a 15 percent tax on the excess. The success penalty is covered in more detail in Chapter 14.

───────────────▶ ACTION ITEM ◀───────────────

If you are receiving, over the course of 1 year, more than $150,000 from retirement plans ($750,000, if the distribution is a lump sum), talk to your retirement plan administrator to see whether there are ways to receive less income and avoid the 15 percent penalty tax.

───

When I die, what happens to my TSA?

At your death, your beneficiary receives the full value of your TSA, unless you have specifically requested that the distributions be made in installments. If a lump-sum distribution is received by a spouse, all or part of it may be rolled over into an IRA within 60 days of the date of distribution. The first $5,000 of a TSA may be distributed tax-free to a beneficiary. Otherwise, all amounts received by a beneficiary will be taxable as income.

POINTS TO REMEMBER

▶ To qualify for TSA contributions, you must be employed by a special category of employer, usually a school or a tax-exempt organization.

▶ TSA contributions must be invested with an insurance company or a mutual fund.

▶ Generally, the maximum contribution amount is $9,500 a year, and it must be made entirely through payroll deductions.

▶ You may change your TSA contribution amount only once per calendar year.

▶ You may borrow up to half the value of your TSA, but interest is not deductible.

▶ There is no special tax treatment available when you withdraw your money from your TSA. TSA withdrawals are always considered ordinary income.

9

Employee Stock Ownership Plan (ESOP)

*W*ant to give employees a reason for working harder and better? Let them own part of the company! That's what the ESOP, or employee stock ownership plan, is all about.

The philosophy may be simple, but the ESOP is the most unusual of all the retirement plans. It allows employees to purchase a portion of the company they work for, while allowing employers to sell a part of their company without paying taxes!

ALL ABOUT ESOPs

ESOPs have many purposes, ranging from preventing hostile takeovers to increasing productivity and profitability. Their primary use is to transfer ownership of a company to its employees by either giving them or allowing them to purchase shares of the company's stock. This transfer allows employers to sell all, or mostly all, of their business and still retain an element of control.

Over the past few years, some large corporations have disbanded and distributed their ESOP plans as a result of tax law changes that made them obsolete. Other ESOPs, however, are alive and well. The potential confusion results from the fact that there are two kinds of ESOPs.

The first type of ESOP, based on a tax credit, was eliminated in 1986. By 1988, most companies had phased-out these plans by distributing the accumulated shares of stock to their employees.

EMPLOYEE STOCK OWNERSHIP PLAN (ESOP) OVERVIEW

Status While Working

Employer and employee contribute to purchase company stock. Maximum: 15% of income up to $30,000; employee's share maximum: $8,728 (1992).

Dividends distributed each year, taxable as ordinary income.

After age 55, choice of other investments.

Effects of Leaving Employer

Vested over time, up to 7 years. Vested portion may be held for up to 5 years before payout starts.

May take out stock or cash.

Tax due on basis of stock or current market value. Lump-sum treatment may apply.

Roll over to IRA or trustee-to-trustee transfer possible.

Penalty for early distribution, if under age 59½.

Effects of Withdrawal While Working

Usually not possible, but if employer allows it, distribution will be taxable with penalty if employee under age 59½.

Tax due on basis of stock or current market value.

Special Circumstances

Disability

Account becomes fully vested.

Distributions at any age not subject to early distribution penalty, but fully taxable.

Distributions may not begin for up to 5 years, and may spread over another 5 years.

Roll over to IRA or trustee-to-trustee transfer.

Lump sum eligible for special averaging.

Retirement

Account becomes fully vested.

Receive full value of account within 1 year, as stock or as cash.

Distributions taxed as ordinary income, unless received as lump sum. Lump sum is eligible for special averaging.

Distribution may be rolled over to IRA; if stock, find a trustee that accepts stock; otherwise, sell and transfer proceeds within 60-day period.

Death

Account becomes fully vested and goes to beneficiary. May be a delay of up to 5 years before distribution starts.

Spouse may take lump sum with special averaging or roll into own IRA within 5 years.

Other beneficiaries must pay taxes at ordinary income rates.

First $5,000 may be tax-free.

A second kind of ESOP, the leveraged ESOP, is still available and becoming more popular. Its popularity is growing, first, because owners want employees to help prevent hostile takeovers, and, second, because some owners and employees believe that an ESOP will increase productivity through pride of ownership.

THE LEVERAGED ESOP

The leveraged ESOP is a retirement plan that fits the general definition of a defined-contribution retirement plan; that is, there are contribution limitations, vesting requirements, withdrawal restrictions, and so on. However, instead of investing in a variety of investments, as do other retirement plans, the ESOP invests primarily in shares of the company's stock.

The term "leveraged" refers to the way the company buys the stock that goes into the plan. The ESOP borrows money and uses that money to purchase the stock. The company pays the loan back over the years, from its cash flow. Because the company can deduct much of the interest on the loan, plus the value of the stock going into the plan, the leveraged ESOP offers important tax advantages.

For owners of a nonpublicly traded company (the shares of stock are not traded on a stock exchange), the ESOP offers a way to sell portions of their company over time. Additionally, owners can defer tax liability on the gain from the sale by purchasing a qualified replacement property (QRP). This QRP can be the stock of most publicly traded U.S. corporations.

Even though the leveraged ESOP has advantages, not all companies decide to borrow to establish an ESOP. Many companies, especially the larger, publicly traded ones, prefer to buy the stock with cash.

As an employee/shareholder in a nonpublicly traded ESOP, you usually have the right to vote only to approve or disapprove a corporate merger, sale, or liquidation. You may find you have only one vote, regardless of the number of shares you own. If your ESOP shares are publicly traded, usually each share of stock you own gives you one vote, and you may vote on all corporate matters brought before the shareholders.

ESOPs FOR OWNERS

For owners of nonpublicly traded companies, an ESOP offers a particularly good way to "cash out" of (sell) the business without having to "go public" with the company. As you might guess, however, there are many ins and outs to arranging this kind of ESOP sale. Competent legal and accounting help is essential. Let's look briefly at this process.

Under IRS rules, an owner of a nonpublicly traded company must sell at least 30 percent of the company to the ESOP, in order to get significant tax advantages. Having sold at least 30 percent, the owner can take those cash proceeds and invest them, tax-deferred, in any U.S. stock (a QRP). There are restrictions as to the type of QRP allowed, but investing in a balanced portfolio of low-yielding growth stocks, with the intention of holding on to them for long-term appreciation, will usually qualify. On the other hand, an owner who wants cash without incurring a taxable event could invest entirely in bonds and then use the bonds as collateral for a loan. Borrowing against a QRP is not considered a taxable event. At death, the heirs receive the QRP without having to pay capital gains tax.

Given the considerable income tax benefits and the estate planning benefits for owners of businesses, we expect to see more ESOPs in the future.

ESOPs FOR EMPLOYEES

An ESOP can be a good deal for employees, too. It allows them to become owners and to participate in a company's long-term growth, tax-deferred, by acquiring shares of the company through a retirement plan. Often, employers simply give shares to employees as a reward for longevity with the company. Let's look in greater detail at how this works.

If your employer establishes an ESOP, you generally get shares of stock when the company deposits the shares into the plan and you become vested. As with other retirement plans, ESOPs usually use the standard 5-to-7-year vesting rules, although some plans vest immediately.

Many ESOPs allow employee contributions. If you have this kind of plan, you can designate a certain percentage of your income to buy shares. Often, employers match some or all of these contributions; that is, for every dollar you contribute to an ESOP, your employer might contribute 5 cents, 30 cents, or even another dollar!

There are contribution limitations. As in most other retirement plans, the maximum contribution you and your employer can make to an ESOP is the lesser of 25 percent of your income or $30,000.

For nonpublicly traded companies, the price of the shares should be determined by a reputable accounting firm, although no accounting firm will guarantee share price or state what the company would actually sell for, if it were placed on the auction block. Accountants will give only a reasonable estimate of the company's value.

Publicly traded companies, when contributing shares to an ESOP, generally use the market value of the shares—the share price on a particular day or an average of several days' prices. If employee contributions are allowed, many companies allow share purchases at a slight discount (ranging from 1 to 15 percent) from market value. In this way, employees can pay less to buy the shares.

DISTRIBUTIONS AND BORROWING

While you are working, if your employer allows it, you may receive a distribution from the ESOP, but it will be taxable. If the distribution occurs before age 59½, you may be subject to an early distribution penalty.

If you receive a distribution in shares of stock, you can choose to figure your taxes based on what the company paid for the stock, not on its current market value. When you eventually sell the stock, you will be responsible for taxes on the rest of the value.

If you want, you can choose the market value of the stock as of the distribution date, to calculate your taxes.

Borrowing from an ESOP is not allowed.

──────────────▶ **ACTION ITEM** ◀──────────────

The tax issues surrounding a distribution from an ESOP can be very complicated. Consult with a tax professional, to determine the optimum withdrawal method and to help you avoid penalties.

LEAVING THE COMPANY BEFORE YOU RETIRE

If you leave your company, your ESOP account will be distributed to you, but maybe not immediately. Current rules allow ESOPs to postpone distribution up to 5 years after an employee leaves a job. Moreover, when the distribution begins, it may take the form of an installment distribution lasting another 5 years.

Because it can take up to 5 years to receive a distribution from an ESOP, the value of your stock will be established when you leave the company. You will be entitled to receive at least that amount, even though it may be over a period of time. At the time you leave the company, you may choose to receive either stock or cash.

→ **ACTION ITEM** ←

If you are participating in an ESOP and thinking of leaving your employment, check with your ESOP administrator, to be sure you understand how long it will take for your ESOP account to be distributed to you, and what form of payment (cash or shares) you should expect.

GETTING MONEY OUT OF AN ESOP AT RETIREMENT

When you retire, you will receive your ESOP account value within one year. If you choose, you may receive a lump-sum distribution (either in shares of stock or, if you choose, in cash), which you can then roll over into an IRA or keep and pay the taxes. Lump-sum distributions from an ESOP are eligible for special tax rates.

You may also elect to have the ESOP paid out over time—say, over 5 years—but receiving your payout over time makes you ineligible for special tax treatment.

If you are close to retirement, you have to be concerned about the value of your ESOP. It is possible that, when you retire, the stock's value could be down. However, a new rule protects you. When you reach age 55, with at least 10 years of service, the ESOP must be expanded to allow you to diversify 25 percent of your account into other investments. You must be given at least 3 investment choices. When you reach 60, the plan must allow up to 50 percent of your account to be diversified.

This means you can make investments that may not be as volatile as your company stock. It also means you will have to make some investment decisions!

➔ **ACTION ITEM** ◆

If you are at least age 55, evaluate other investment options within your ESOP. You may wish to diversify your investments in order to meet other goals, such as safety and liquidity.

Is an ESOP risky?

If an ESOP is your only retirement plan, then you need to be concerned about "putting all your eggs in one basket." After all, you are working for the company; your regular income depends on its success. If your retirement security also depends on the company's success, then you need to be very sure the company will do well!

➔ **ACTION ITEM** ◆

If you are offered the opportunity to participate in an ESOP, make investments outside the company, too. Don't put all your retirement eggs in one basket!

What happens to dividends paid by the ESOP?

You will probably receive, by check, the dividends on your shares in the ESOP. They may be paid out monthly, but, most often, ESOPs send shareholders their dividends once a year.

You will pay taxes on these dividends, just as you would on other dividends. However, there is no early distribution penalty on dividends paid from an ESOP.

May I borrow from my ESOP?

Borrowing from an ESOP is not allowed.

─────────────────→ ACTION ITEM ←─────────────────

Count as taxable income all dividends you receive from an ESOP, making sure the appropriate income taxes are paid on time. You don't want to be underwithheld at tax time!

Is there special lump-sum tax treatment on ESOPs?

If the ESOP is distributed as a lump sum in one calendar year, it may be eligible for special tax treatment.

Do IRA rollover rules apply to ESOPs?

Yes. You can postpone taxes, if you receive at least 50 percent of the account value, by rolling an ESOP distribution into an IRA within 60 days of the date of distribution.

Be careful if you are receiving stock: not all IRA trustees allow stock in their IRA accounts. Shop among brokerage firms and independent trustees, before taking a distribution in stock from your ESOP.

What happens if I delay receiving a distribution from the ESOP?

If you reach age 70½ and don't take the required distribution from your ESOP, you may face a penalty for late distribution. This penalty may be as high as 50 percent of the amount that should have been distributed!

─────────────────→ ACTION ITEM ←─────────────────

If you anticipate receiving a large distribution of stock or cash from your ESOP or you delay receipt of the ESOP, check with a tax professional to be sure you understand the penalties that may be imposed on excess benefits or late distributions.

What withdrawal penalties from the ESOP do I need to watch for?

If you receive a distribution before age 59¹/₂, an early distribution penalty may apply. If too much money is distributed to you at once, a success penalty may also apply.

Does the success penalty apply to ESOP plans?

If you receive a distribution in one year of more than $150,000 ($750,000, if the distribution is a lump sum) from retirement plans, you may have to pay a 15 percent penalty tax on the excess. The success penalty is covered in more detail in Chapter 14.

───────────────→ **ACTION ITEM** ←───────────────

If you are receiving more than $150,000 from all retirement plans in one year ($750,000, if the distribution is a lump sum), talk to your retirement plan administrator to see whether there are ways to receive less income and avoid the 15 percent penalty tax.

Do the social security integration rules apply to ESOPs?

No. An ESOP cannot be integrated with social security. (For more information on social security integration, read Chapter 12.)

What happens to my ESOP if I die or become disabled?

As with other retirement plans, your vested ESOP will be distributed to your named beneficiary in the event of your death, or to you if you are disabled, free of early distribution penalty. If the beneficiary is your spouse, he or she will have the same choices for IRA rollover or special averaging of any lump-sum distribution that you would have had. If your beneficiary receives stock, the same tax choices apply that you would have had. The first $5,000 of the distribution may be tax-free to your beneficiary.

Unlike other retirement plans, upon your death or disability, the ESOP is not required to make a distribution within 1 year. The plan has up to 5 years to begin making a distribution and can pay it out over another 5 years.

POINTS TO REMEMBER

▸ The tax credit ESOP has been phased out; the leveraged ESOP is alive and well.

▸ If you are an owner, you may use the ESOP to "cash out" of (sell) your business without having to go public.

▸ If you are an employee, your participation in an ESOP means you gain ownership of your company by owning shares.

▸ Your shares will probably become fully vested within a maximum of 7 years.

▸ Employees may be given, or may purchase, their shares. Often, the company will match employee purchases.

▸ Dividends from an ESOP are taxable.

▸ Be sensitive to putting "all your eggs in one basket," when you participate in an ESOP.

▸ Distributions from an ESOP, whether you leave the company or retire, may not be immediate.

10

Self-Employed Retirement Plan (Keogh)

*R*etirement plans for self-employed people and their employees have joined the ranks of regular corporate plans. Upgrades by Congress in recent years have made these self-employed plans "look and feel" much like corporate retirement plans, starting with the name. Today, although still informally known as "Keoghs" and "HR-10s," they are more accurately known as noncorporate retirement plans.

A Keogh (let's be informal!) allows self-employed people to make a tax-deductible contribution to their own retirement plan and to their employees' plans.

This chapter starts with qualifying for a Keogh and then explains the mechanics of calculating the contribution and deduction.

QUALIFYING FOR A KEOGH

Determining whether you qualify for a Keogh is not difficult. To qualify, you must simply be self-employed, which means you conduct a trade or business full-time or part-time. Your business must not be incorporated. Partners in a business such as a law firm or medical facility may be eligible for a Keogh.

As a self-employed person, you are eligible for retirement plans other than a Keogh. Don't overlook alternatives such as an individual retirement account (IRA) or a simplified employee pension (SEP). We recommend that you review all three before you decide which one you will use.

SELF-EMPLOYED RETIREMENT PLAN (KEOGH) OVERVIEW

Status While Working

Employer contributes up to 25% of "net" income or $30,000 under defined-contribution method.

Contributions may be based on profits only.

May contribute to target retirement amount under defined-benefit method.

Employer determines available investments.

Employer may be trustee.

Owner is employee.

Effects of Leaving Employer

Employees vested over time, up to 7 years. May not contribute unless self-employed.

May borrow. (See Effects of Withdrawal While Working.)

Eligible for 10-year or 5-year special averaging, if plan is terminated.

Roll over to IRA or trustee-to-trustee transfer anytime.

Withdrawals before age 59½ subject to early distribution penalty, unless taken over lifetime or retiring and at least age 55.

Money withdrawn (not borrowed), at any age, taxed as ordinary income. (See Effects of Withdrawal While Working.)

Effects of Withdrawal While Working

Nonowner-employee may borrow from vested portion. Owner may not borrow.

Borrowed funds must be repaid in quarterly payments within 5 years. The period may be longer, if buying a home.

Interest is not deductible.

Money withdrawn (not borrowed) prior to age 59½ subject to early distribution penalty, unless received over life expectancy.

Money withdrawn (not borrowed), at any age, taxed as ordinary income.

Special Circumstances

Disability

Account becomes fully vested.

Distributions at any age not subject to early distribution penalty.

Distributions taxed.

May borrow. (See Effects of Withdrawal While Working.)

Contributions stop.

Roll over to an IRA or trustee-to-trustee transfer anytime.

Eligible for 10-year or 5-year special averaging.

Retirement

Account becomes fully vested.

All distributions (not borrowed) taxed as ordinary income, unless received as lump sum.

Distributions before age 55 subject to early distribution penalty, unless taken over time.

Must begin distribution by age 70½.

Eligible for 10-year or 5-year special averaging.

Roll over to an IRA or trustee-to-trustee transfer anytime.

> *Death*
> Account becomes fully vested and goes to beneficiary.
> Beneficiary may be able to use 10-year or 5-year special averaging.
> If payout has started, beneficiary must continue payout.
> If payout has not started, spouse may roll over to IRA within 5 years.
> Other beneficiaries must take distribution within 5 years or over life expectancy.
> All distributions taxed as ordinary income unless received as lump sum. First $5,000 is tax-free to beneficiary.
> Early distribution penalty not applicable to beneficiaries.

⟶ ACTION ITEM ⟵

Determine whether your involvement with a trade or business makes you eligible for a Keogh. The easiest way to do this is to check with a tax professional. Find out whether you can file Schedule C, Profit or Loss From Business, when you file your income taxes.

TYPES OF KEOGH PLANS

As with corporate plans, there are two basic types of Keogh plans: a *defined-contribution* Keogh plan and a *defined-benefit* Keogh plan. These plans are very different from each other; each has its own advantages and benefits. The reasons you would contribute to one rather than the other are very different. Let's take a close look at each.

DEFINED-CONTRIBUTION KEOGH PLAN

A defined-contribution Keogh plan is an agreement to do one of the following:

▶ Regardless of profit, set aside a specific percent of income each year (a money-purchase plan);

▶ Contribute to your (and your employees') retirement, based usually on profit (a profit-sharing plan);

▶ Use a combination of profit-sharing and money-purchase plans.

Notice that the names of these defined-contribution Keogh plans are the same as their corporate counterparts. However, contribution amounts to Keoghs are determined quite differently from those made to corporate plans, and this is the big difference between them. Generally, Keoghs use a *net income method* to determine contributions; corporate plans use an *income method*. Keogh contributions must be deducted *before* they can be calculated; corporate contributions need not be deducted to be calculated. Because of this difference, a decision to incorporate and use a corporate retirement plan could put more money in your pocket.

Sound confusing? The bottom line is: you end up contributing less to a Keogh plan. We'll discuss exactly how this works, a little later. First, let's look more closely at the defined-contribution Keogh, starting with the money-purchase plan.

MONEY-PURCHASE KEOGH PLAN

A money-purchase Keogh plan is a defined-contribution retirement plan. It *requires* the self-employed person to contribute a specific percent of net income to the plan each year. The maximum contribution is 25 percent or up to $30,000.

The contribution percentage is established when the money-purchase plan is originally set up. The *percent* of contribution does not change from year to year, even though income may go up and down.

WEALTH   *Forced Savings.* Ken's tax preparation business is a
BUILDING   moonlighting job. By day he works as an engineer,
PROFILE   and in the evening he prepares tax returns. He has a
                    small but growing clientele. He'll retire from his day-
time job in 20 years, with a nice pension. The moonlighting income is extra, and he has been spending it on "vacations and toys."

Because his savings habits are not too good, Ken decides to set up a money-purchase Keogh to force him to save a percentage of his moonlighting income. The forced savings, he figures, will make his retirement income "just that much more." "Who knows," he says, "with this added retirement savings, I might even be able to retire early!"

─────────────▶ ACTION ITEM ◀─────────────

If you are planning to retire after age 60, you are now younger than age 50, and your self-employed business is steady or growing, consider using a money-purchase Keogh as a forced retirement savings plan.

Because the contributions to a money-purchase plan are required, you have to be careful not to commit to a percentage contribution greater than the amount you can handle. If you suffer an economic hardship by making the required contribution, the IRS may allow you to postpone your contribution for a year, and possibly longer. However, you must eventually make up all contributions, plus what they would have earned during the time they were postponed. Alternatively, you may increase or decrease your percentage contribution by filing amendments to the plan. To stop contributions altogether, you may terminate the plan.

PROFIT-SHARING KEOGH PLAN

A profit-sharing Keogh is a defined-contribution retirement plan that allows a self-employed person to contribute, on an *optional* basis, up to 15 percent of net income (but no more than $30,000) to the retirement plan.

─────────────▶ ACTION ITEM ◀─────────────

If your income is subject to large annual swings and you cannot be certain that you will have enough money for a Keogh contribution, consider using a profit-sharing Keogh. All contributions to this type of Keogh are optional.

In a profit-sharing Keogh, your contribution *percent* can change from year to year. It can range from 0 to 15 percent. There is no requirement to make a contribution to the plan.

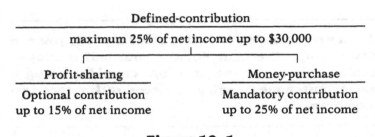

Figure 10–1
Defined-contribution plans.

Figure 10–1 puts defined-contribution profit-sharing and money-purchase plans side-by-side, for comparison.

NET INCOME

As mentioned earlier, the primary difference between corporate re-tirement plans and Keogh plans is in the way contributions are deter-mined. Corporate plans use contributions based on income; Keoghs use net income. This means that Keogh contributions must be de-ducted before they can be calculated. Thus, contributions to Keoghs will be less than contributions to similar corporate retirement plans.

Net income is income *after* you have deducted the retirement plan contribution; that is, if you treat the 15 percent contribution as a deduction, your actual contribution is only 13.043 percent. Similarly, if the 25 percent contribution is deducted, your actual contribution is only 20 percent.

The formula for your net contribution looks like this:

$$\frac{\text{income} \times \text{percent contribution}}{1 + \text{percent contribution}} = \text{contribution amount}$$

If we assume the self-employed person's income is $10,000, the contri-bution amount would be:

$$\frac{\$10,000 \times .15}{1.15} = \$1,304$$

$1,304 is 13.04 percent of $10,000, but it is 15 percent of $8,696 ($10,000 − $1,304).

Under a similar corporate retirement plan, the contribution would be $1,500, a $196 advantage. Over 30 years, assuming steady contributions of $1,500 per year earning 8 percent, the corporate retirement plan would be worth nearly $170,000. The Keogh, at the same interest rate, with its $1,304 annual contribution, would be worth about $148,000, a $22,000 difference!

WEALTH BUILDING PROFILE *Figuring the Amount.* Alison is a self-employed real estate agent. She figures that, last year, after paying all business expenses, her profit was $25,000.

If she wants to make a 15 percent contribution to a profit-sharing Keogh plan, she first deducts the contribution, $3,260 ($25,000 × 13.043%), and arrives at $21,739 of net profit.

Her contribution of $3,260 is 15 percent of $21,739.

For defined-contribution Keoghs, the maximum you may contribute is 25 percent of net income or up to $30,000. You can accomplish this in two ways:

▶ Set up two defined-contribution Keoghs—a money-purchase Keogh, allowing contributions up to 10 percent of net income, and a profit-sharing Keogh, allowing contributions up to 15 percent of net income;

▶ Set up one money-purchase Keogh and contribute 25 percent of net income.

As an alternative, defined-benefit Keoghs may allow you to contribute much more.

DEFINED-BENEFIT KEOGH PLAN

A defined-benefit Keogh plan allows you to decide the amount of your retirement income. The plan allows you to make contributions to meet that goal. To meet your retirement income goal, you may be able to claim a larger deduction than would have been available under a defined-contribution Keogh.

Defined-benefit Keoghs work particularly well for people who are close to retirement because they allow "catching up" for lost time. It is not unheard of to catch up by contributing as much as 70 percent of annual income to this plan.

The maximum retirement income you can currently plan for under a defined-benefit Keogh is the lesser of $112,221 (1992) or 100 percent of the average of the three highest consecutive years of income while you are in the plan.

The accumulated money within your defined-benefit Keogh cannot be greater than an amount needed to produce a maximum income of $112,221 per year for the rest of your life (this exact amount adjusts each year because of inflation).

To determine the amount needed within the plan, to produce this income, is another matter. There are many variables. For example, you don't know how long you are going to live, nor do you know what interest rate you will be receiving on the money. These variables (and others) require the help of an actuary, to determine your maximum annual contribution to the plan.

COMPARING KEOGH PLANS

Figure 10–2 illustrates the primary differences between defined-benefit Keoghs and defined-contribution Keoghs. The important point to remember about a defined-contribution Keogh is that your income determines the annual contribution amount. The value of your Keogh at retirement will be the amount of your annual contributions plus the accumulated interest, dividends, or capital gains.

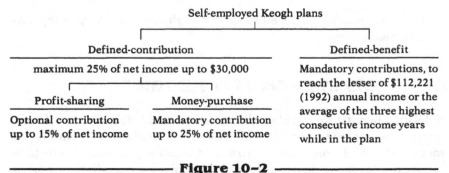

Figure 10–2
Comparison of Keogh contributions.

Under a defined-benefit Keogh, your retirement income is determined before you retire. While you are working, you identify a *specific amount* of income you would like to receive at retirement. An actuary will then determine the annual contribution you need to deposit each year, to meet this goal. Once you reach this goal, no new contributions can be made.

▶ ACTION ITEM ◀

If you are self-employed and well into your career, consider using a defined-benefit Keogh to maximize your retirement contributions. To set up this plan, you may need to consult with retirement planning experts.

WEALTH BUILDING PROFILE *Target Retirement.* Andy is aiming at retirement from his appliance repair business 15 years from now. He sets up a target retirement age of 65 and a target annual income from a retirement plan of $12,000. With this income plus his income from social security and the sale of his business, Andy calculates that he will have more than enough to live on. His current income from the repair business is $20,000, which isn't likely to change.

From talking to a retirement specialist, he learns that he will have to accumulate about $115,000, to reach his annual income goal of $12,000 for life. To accumulate $115,000, he must save $4,661 a year and earn 6 percent interest on the money.

The retirement specialist points out that a money-purchase Keogh or profit-sharing Keogh will only allow him to save 20 percent of his income, or $4,000 annually (25 percent of his net income). Only a defined-benefit Keogh will allow him to save the full $4,661 per year.

Andy will have to tighten his spending belt to meet his goal, but he knows he can do it.

Even if your income is small from your self-employed business, it still makes sense for you to set up a Keogh. The government allows you to contribute enough money to a defined-benefit Keogh to receive an annual minimum retirement income of $10,000, even though the average of your three highest earning years may be less than $10,000. This means that you may be able to contribute all, or almost all, of your self-employed income to the Keogh. You must start young, though; in order to achieve this goal, you have to be in the defined-benefit Keogh for at least 10 years. Otherwise, for each year short of 10, the $10,000 is reduced by one-tenth.

If you are the owner of more than one business and intend to make retirement plan contributions, you must lump your plans together and treat them as one plan.

ESTABLISHING A KEOGH PLAN

To establish a Keogh plan during a specific year, you must complete the appropriate forms and open up an account at a financial institution *no later than year-end*. Most often, Keoghs are set up through savings institutions, mutual funds, or insurance or trust companies.

WEALTH BUILDING PROFILE   *Talking to the Right Person at the Right Time.* Marsha made enough money in her pet-sitting business during the year to think about contributing to a Keogh plan. At 36, she thought it was high time to start doing something about retirement. With Christmas and the holiday rush, however, December did not seem to be a good month to start. After all, she knew she had until "tax time" to put the money in the plan. "Why worry about it in December?" she asked herself.

Fortunately for her, she happened to be talking to an alert bank teller while making a deposit late in December. The teller correctly informed her that the plan had to be established by December 31. Contributions could be made later.

Marsha walked straight over to the New Accounts desk, filled out the paperwork, and immediately established a plan with a minimum deposit of $10.

Now that the account is established, she has until the due date of her tax return, including extensions, to contribute the full amount.

If you do not establish a Keogh by year-end, you cannot contribute to it. However, you may be allowed to contribute to an IRA or SEP.

─────────────→ **ACTION ITEM** ←─────────────

If you expect to start a Keogh this year, consider your age and your ability to make future contributions. Then determine the best type of Keogh for your needs. This should be done *well before year-end!*

MAKING CONTRIBUTIONS

A Keogh must be *established* by year-end. To claim a tax deduction, however, your *contribution* need not be made until your income tax return is filed. If you file for extensions, you might have up to 8½ months after year-end to make your contribution! This means you could have until September 15 to contribute and still take a deduction for the previous tax year.

If you have already established a defined-benefit or money-purchase Keogh, new rules say that you must make quarterly contributions, on April 15, July 15, October 15, and January 15. Contributions to established profit-sharing Keoghs, however, do not have to be made until your tax return deadline (with extensions, not later than 8½ months from your plan's year-end).

You lose an advantage if you don't contribute to a Keogh as early in the year as possible. Contributing early allows your money to compound tax-deferred for the full year. This may not sound like much, but, depending on the amount you are contributing, early deposits may end up increasing your Keogh by several thousand dollars!

Table 10–1 compares an annual $4,000 Keogh contribution made at the beginning of the year with one made at the end of the year. Each account earns 6 percent interest.

Because of the advantages of investing early in the year, try not to let current cash shortages deter you from making contributions to your Keogh. If you are lacking cash, you can contribute borrowed money from a bank loan, or noncash assets such as stocks or bonds. The tax aspects of contributing something other than cash are quite

Table 10-1
Why Contribute Early?

Year	Contribution Made on Jan. 1 of Each Year (End-of-Year Values)	Contribution Made on Dec. 31 of Each Year (End-of-Year Values)
1	4,240	4,000
2	8,734	8,240
3	13,498	12,734
4	18,548	17,498
5	23,900	22,548
10	55,886	52,724
20	155,970	147,142

complicated. You should seek professional tax help before attempting a noncash contribution.

If, by chance, you contribute more than the rules allow, you will have made an overcontribution. Overcontributions to a Keogh are subject to an annual 6 percent excise tax, unless you withdraw the overcontribution amount and all its earnings before the due date of the tax return. Additionally, all *earnings* on this excess contribution, besides being taxed, will be subject to an early distribution penalty if you are younger than 59$^1/_2$.

---------------→ ACTION ITEM ←---------------

Contribute to a Keogh as much as you can afford, and do it as early in the year as possible. Don't let a temporary cash shortage delay your Keogh contribution. Find ways to borrow money or talk to a tax professional about possible ways you can contribute noncash assets.

KEOGHS AND YOUR EMPLOYEES

As with any retirement plan, if you have employees, you must contribute to their plan too. Generally, the same vesting and participation rules that apply to corporate plans also apply to Keoghs. You may require up to one year of service before your employees become eligible, and you can have up to 7 years as your vesting schedule. Or, you could require 2 years of service for eligibility, with all future contributions 100 percent vested.

You can exclude from your Keogh all part-time employees (those working less than 1,000 hours per year), those under 21, and all union employees. These individuals should explore contributing to an IRA.

Employees who were once working full-time and are now working part-time may be the employees for whom the Keogh was originally established. They will continue to move up the vesting ladder, even though they are now working part-time (more than 500 hours, but less than 1,000 hours per year). New contributions to the Keogh, however, will probably not be made for them. If they are working less than 500 hours, they may have a "break in service" and should talk to a retirement plan administrator.

———————→ ACTION ITEM ←———————

If you are self-employed and have employees, verify from your employees' records those who are eligible to receive a Keogh contribution. If you are an employee, check with your employer to determine plan eligibility requirements.

GETTING MONEY OUT
BEFORE RETIREMENT

There are only two ways to get money out of a Keogh prior to retirement: borrowing or taking a distribution. Generally, owner/employees may not borrow from a Keogh. However, other participants, such as nonowner-employees, may be allowed to borrow up to 50 percent of their account value at competitive interest rates! Keep in mind that not all plans allow borrowing.

If your Keogh plan allows you to borrow, the rules say you must pay the money back in equal payments, at least quarterly, and the loan must be repaid within 5 years. Repayment of a loan used to buy a principal residence may be extended beyond 5 years. Your employer may require you to use payroll withholding to pay back the loan. If you leave your job, your employer may demand full and immediate repayment.

The interest you pay is not deductible.

Distributions are the second way to get money out of a Keogh, but taking a distribution prior to age 59½ can be an expensive way to get money. You will have to pay an early distribution penalty, along with income taxes. You should avoid this penalty if at all possible. Consider borrowing, not distribution, if you are under age 59½.

However, if you are older than 59½, you (whether you're an employee or an owner-employee) may take withdrawals from your Keogh while you are still working, without paying an early distribution penalty. Remember, though: the withdrawals will be taxed as ordinary income unless the account is distributed under the lump-sum distribution rules.

Before borrowing from any retirement plan, consult a tax professional and be sure you understand all of the loan conditions, such as how and when the money must be repaid.

GETTING MONEY OUT
AT RETIREMENT

At retirement, you have several choices: take the money from your Keogh as a lump sum and pay taxes at the special tax rate; have it distributed to you over a period of years; or roll it into an IRA and delay taxes. At retirement, all employer contributions become fully vested. Moreover, you may have the chance to leave the money with the plan until you are ready, or required, to withdraw it.

You can get your money out of a Keogh, penalty-free, as long as you are at least age 55 and you retire. If you haven't retired, you must terminate the plan.

To avoid the early distribution penalty before age 55, you must terminate the plan and take the distribution from your Keogh as a *series of payments based on your life expectancy* (or your and your spouse's life expectancies). This method avoids an early withdrawal penalty, but it doesn't avoid taxes. To avoid taxes *and* penalty, roll the entire amount into an IRA.

If I decide to incorporate, what do I do with my Keogh plan?

If you decide to incorporate and start a corporate retirement plan, you can terminate the Keogh and transfer the assets to your new corporate plan. Or, your Keogh can be "frozen": it can remain as a Keogh, but no new contributions can be made to it.

Your Keogh can also be rolled into an IRA. The rollover IRA will never enjoy special tax treatment for distributions, but you can avoid the annual tax return that the Keogh requires.

If I first start out with a defined-contribution Keogh plan, can I later switch to a defined-benefit Keogh plan?

Yes. If you start out with either a defined-contribution Keogh or a defined-benefit Keogh, you can later switch to the other. However, if you switch to a defined-benefit Keogh, previous contributions to Keoghs may cause your future Keogh contributions to be reduced.

Can my Keogh plan be integrated with social security?

Yes. Your Keogh and social security could be considered one program, even though the government will pay the social security check to you separately. For a broader explanation of social security integration, see Chapter 12.

―――――――――――――→ **ACTION ITEM** ←―――――――――――――

Check to see whether your employer uses social security to determine, in part, your retirement benefit.

Must I have a trustee for my Keogh plan?

Yes. However, *you* may be the trustee of your own Keogh. Being your own trustee and not paying trustee fees will save you money!

As a self-employed person, am I restricted solely to using Keogh plans?

No. A Keogh is only one of three plans available for self-employed individuals and their employees. The other two are an individual retirement account (IRA) and a simplified employee pension (SEP) plan. The rules are quite different for each of these plans, and the advantages of contributions to these plans may change your thinking regarding contributions to Keoghs. We recommend that you read about IRAs and SEPs before you decide among the available options.

How will a distribution from my Keogh plan be affected as a result of a divorce or disability?

If a distribution is made to a nonparticipant, such as an ex-spouse, as a result of a qualified domestic relations order (QDRO), or to a participant as a result of total disability, there is never an early distribution penalty. However, unless the distribution is rolled into an IRA, it will be taxed to the person receiving it.

When *must* I begin distributions from my Keogh plan?

You must begin withdrawing money from your Keogh on April 1 of the year *after* you reach age 70$^{1}/_{2}$. At that time, the IRS requires distribution of interest and principal to begin. If you do not withdraw the proper amount, the IRS can penalize you up to 50 percent of the amount that you should have withdrawn!

Can creditors get at my Keogh?

Only the federal government, to collect back taxes, and an ex-spouse, under a qualified domestic relations order (QDRO), can attach your Keogh. Other than these two exceptions, as long as funds are not withdrawn, your Keogh is judgment-proof.

Does the success penalty apply to Keogh plans?

If you receive a distribution of more than $150,000 per year ($750,000, if the distribution is one lump sum) from retirement plans, you may have to pay a 15 percent penalty tax on the excess. The success penalty is covered in more detail in Chapter 14.

─────────────────→ **ACTION ITEM** ←─────────────────

If you are receiving, from all retirement plans, more than $150,000 annually ($750,000, if the distribution is one lump sum), talk to your retirement plan administrator to see whether there are ways to receive less income, to avoid the 15 percent penalty tax.

If I have a retirement plan with my current employer and I set up a side business, can I contribute to a Keogh plan?

If you are a nonowner-employee of a business that has a retirement plan, and you also have a self-employed business, you may contribute to a Keogh based on your self-employed earnings.

If I die before distribution begins, what choices does my beneficiary have?

If your beneficiary is your spouse, he or she has the same choices you would have had if you had withdrawn the money: IRA rollover, special tax treatment *if you would have been eligible*, or annuity payout. If your beneficiary is not a spouse, that person, regardless of how the money is received, will always pay ordinary income taxes on it.

The first $5,000 distributed from a Keogh to a beneficiary is free of taxes, and there is never an early distribution penalty to a beneficiary.

──────── POINTS TO REMEMBER ────────

▸ Keogh plans are for the self-employed. Recent legislative changes have caused Keoghs to resemble corporate plans.

▸ Like corporate plans, there are two basic types of Keoghs: a defined-contribution plan and a defined-benefit plan.

▸ Contribution amounts are the same as corporate amounts, but are calculated on net income (that is, after the Keogh contribution has been deducted) rather than income.

▸ If you are an employee of a business that has a retirement plan, and you also have a self-employed business, you may contribute to a Keogh based on your self-employed income.

▸ If you have employees, you will be required to cover them under your Keogh, with certain exceptions.

▸ Your Keogh must be established by calendar year-end; your contribution must be made by the time your income tax return is filed, including extensions.

▸ Owner-employees generally may not borrow from their Keogh plans.

▸ When you retire, you may withdraw money from your Keogh starting at age 55. Keoghs enjoy special tax treatment on lump-sum distributions.

11

Simplified Employee Pension (SEP) and Cash or Deferred Arrangement (CODA)

Don't let the odd-sounding names of these retirement plans put you off. They are simply new variations of old themes, created to meet a wider range of employer needs. The SEP and the CODA are specialty retirement plans that are particularly appropriate for the small corporate or self-employed employer.

If your employer is small, or has no retirement plan, read this chapter carefully. You may discover that the SEP or CODA could give you retirement security, new investment opportunities, *and* the chance to save taxes each year!

→ ACTION ITEM ←

If you own or work for a small company, find out whether a SEP-IRA or a CODA-SEP could be added as an employee benefit. You'll need to talk to a retirement plan specialist. Ask your tax preparer or accountant for a recommendation.

Note: **State or local governments and tax-exempt organizations may not offer CODA-SEPs.**

SEPs AND IRAs

A SEP, or simplified employee pension, is both a pension plan and a type of individual retirement account (IRA). Because it is related to both pensions and IRAs, sharing rules from each, it is often called a SEP-IRA.

A SEP-IRA allows employers or self-employed individuals to contribute directly to a retirement plan, for each employee, without the complexities and costs associated with other retirement plans. A SEP-IRA requires only a minimal amount of work to start and maintain. Costs for attorneys or consultants are reduced, if not eliminated.

Another advantage of the SEP is its optional contribution. The employer decides each year whether a contribution to the plan should be made. In this feature, a SEP is similar to a profit-sharing plan. Other plans, such as defined-benefit or money-purchase plans, as discussed earlier, *require* contributions. SEPs allow employees to contribute as though the SEPs were IRAs.

Unlike other retirement plans, a SEP can be set up after the end of the company's tax year (but not after April 15). *Contributions* to the plan need not be made until the due date of the company's tax return, including extensions, which could be up to 8½ months after the plan's year-end!

SEP CONTRIBUTIONS AND VESTING

If your employer establishes a SEP-IRA, most likely your employer will contribute money to it. The amount that can be contributed is determined by your income. If your employer is incorporated, the maximum contribution is the lesser of 15 percent of your income or $30,000. Your employer may contribute less.

If your employer is not a corporation (a noncorporate employer), the contribution, although still made by your employer, will be less. Noncorporate employers must use the net income formula (discussed below), which limits the maximum percentage contribution to 13.043 percent.

If your employer is contributing less than $2,000 (or $2,250 to cover your nonworking spouse) to your SEP, you can make up the difference under the regular and spousal IRA rules. Some or all of your contribution, depending on your income level and whether you or your spouse is a participant in another retirement plan, may be deductible.

SIMPLIFIED EMPLOYEE PENSION (SEP) OVERVIEW

Status While Working

Employer contributes to employee IRA.
Employee may also contribute (may not be able to deduct).
Employer contributions may be up to 15% of income or $30,000.
Employee is limited to $2,000 ($2,500 with spouse).
Employer may determine available investments.
Roll over to another IRA once every 12 months, or trustee-to-trustee transfer anytime.

Effects of Leaving Employer

100% vested at all times.
Roll over to another IRA once every 12 months, or trustee-to-trustee transfer anytime.
Contributions stop.
Withdrawals before age $59\frac{1}{2}$ subject to early distribution penalty, unless taken over lifetime.
Any money withdrawn will be taxed.

Effects of Withdrawal While Working

May not borrow from account.
Any money withdrawn will be taxed.
Money withdrawn prior to age $59\frac{1}{2}$ subject to early distribution penalty, unless received over life expectancy.

Special Circumstances

Disability

Withdrawn money at any age not subject to early distribution penalty.
Any money withdrawn will be taxed.
Contributions stop, unless receiving earned income.
Roll over to another IRA once every 12 months, or trustee-to-trustee transfer anytime.

Retirement

All distributions taxed as ordinary income.
Must begin distributions by age $70\frac{1}{2}$.
Distributions prior to age $59\frac{1}{2}$ subject to early distribution penalty, unless taken over lifetime.
Not eligible for 10-year or 5-year special averaging.

Death

Account goes to beneficiary.
If payout has started, beneficiary must continue payout.
If payout has not started, spouse may roll over to another IRA within 5 years.
Other beneficiaries must take distribution within 5 years or over life expectancy.
All distributions taxed as ordinary income. First $5,000 is tax-free to beneficiary.
Early distribution penalty not applicable to beneficiaries.

All of the money going into a SEP is immediately vested. Your employer cannot discriminate among employees: either your employer contributes for all eligible employees or for none of them. If there is a contribution, the same percentage of income must be contributed for each.

NET INCOME

SEP-IRAs (and Keoghs) are different from corporate retirement plans in the way contributions are determined. Corporate plans use contributions based on income; SEP-IRAs use net income. This means that the SEP-IRA contribution must be deducted before it can be calculated. Thus, contributions to SEP-IRAs will be less than contributions to similar corporate retirement plans.

Net income is the remaining income *after* you have deducted the SEP-IRA contribution. If you treat the 15 percent contribution as a deduction, your actual contribution is only 13.043 percent.

The formula for your net contribution looks like this:

$$\frac{\text{income} \times \text{percent contribution}}{1 + \text{percent contribution}} = \text{contribution amount}$$

(More information on net income is given in Chapter 10.)

QUALIFICATIONS AND EXCLUSIONS

If your employer decides to make no contribution this year, you will be excluded. Your employer may also exclude anyone covered under a collective bargaining agreement.

To receive a contribution from your employer, you must be eligible: at least age 21, employed by this employer for 3 out of the past 5 years, and paid at least $374 by this employer during the year a contribution is made. (The $374 changes each year.)

WEALTH BUILDING PROFILE   *Slowly But Surely.* Rick works for a small automotive repair shop. The employees know each other well, and, with one exception, have been with the company for many years. Even though it is a small shop, they have a retirement plan—a SEP-IRA. Each year, money goes into the plan for their retirement.

This year showed a pretty good profit, and the employees will get a SEP-IRA contribution of 12 percent of their compensation, including overtime. (Andy, who just started this year, won't be eligible to receive a contribution, but he can contribute to an IRA on his own.) Last year's contribution was only 8 percent, but as long as something goes in each year, this plan helps build retirement security. Rick is satisfied to know he's covered by a good plan, even if he does work for a small company.

THE CODA-SEP

The CODA is a SEP-IRA that has been expanded to let you make additional contributions to your retirement plan. It resembles a 401(k) plan and is often called a CODA-SEP.

The contribution amounts for CODAs follow the same rules as 401(k) plans. In 1987, the employee contribution level was set at $7,000. It has changed each year, based on inflation. In 1988, it was raised to $7,313; in 1989, to $7,627; in 1990, to $7,979; in 1991, to $8,475; and in 1992, it is $8,728. In future years, it will rise again. All contributions must be through payroll deduction. (Deductions may be taken only on the first $228,860 of your income.)

Your employer can also contribute to the plan, but your employer's contribution and your contribution combined cannot exceed the lesser of 15 percent of your annual income or $30,000.

If your employer is noncorporate, contributions made by your employer will be subject to the net income calculation, which limits the maximum percentage contribution to 13.043 percent.

CODA ELIGIBILITY

The eligibility rules for CODAs are somewhat different from those for SEP-IRAs. CODAs work fine for employers with few employees or part-time employees. To qualify, your employer must have 25 or fewer eligible employees, and at least 50 percent of these must participate in the plan.

Eligible employees must be at least 21, must have worked for this employer for at least 3 out of the past 5 years, must make more than

CASH OR DEFERRED ARRANGEMENT (CODA) OVERVIEW

Status While Working

Employee contributes percent of salary, up to dollar limit ($8,728 in 1992).

Employer contribution may be up to 15% of income or $30,000.

Employer may determine available investments.

Roll over to another IRA once every 12 months, or trustee-to-trustee transfer anytime.

Effects of Leaving Employer

100% vested at all times.

Roll over to another IRA once every 12 months, or trustee-to-trustee transfer anytime.

Contributions stop.

Withdrawals before age 59½ subject to early distribution penalty, unless received over lifetime.

Any money withdrawn will be taxed.

Effects of Withdrawal While Working

May not borrow from account.

Any money withdrawn will be taxed.

Money withdrawn prior to age 59½ subject to early distribution penalty, unless received over life expectancy.

Special Circumstances

Disability

Withdrawn money, at any age, not subject to early distribution penalty.

Any money withdrawn will be taxed.

Contributions stop, unless receiving earned income.

Roll over to another IRA once every 12 months, or trustee-to-trustee transfer anytime.

Retirement

All distributions taxed as ordinary income.

Must begin distributions by age 70½.

Distributions prior to age 59½ subject to early distribution penalty, unless taken over lifetime.

Not eligible for 10-year or 5-year special averaging.

Death

Account goes to beneficiary.

If payout has started, beneficiary must continue payout.

If payout has not started, spouse may roll over to another IRA within 5 years.

Other beneficiaries must take distribution within 5 years or over life expectancy.

All distributions taxed as ordinary income. First $5,000 is tax-free to beneficiary.

Early distribution penalty not applicable to beneficiaries.

$374 per year, and must not be covered by a collective bargaining agreement. (Eligibility is the same as for SEP-IRAs.)

Although CODAs resemble 401(k) plans, the 401(k) rules allow for any size group. With 401(k)s, eligible employees must be at least 21, must have one year of service, and must have worked at least 1,000 hours within a 12-month period for the same employer.

SEPs AND CODAs
AT RETIREMENT

At retirement, you will have the same distribution options as with a regular IRA. All distributions will be taxed as ordinary income. Lump-sum distributions from SEPs and CODAs do *not* qualify for special tax treatment.

If you retire before age 59$1/2$, watch out for the early distribution penalty. Distributions from SEP-IRAs may begin at any age, without penalty, if you are disabled *or* you receive a series of payments from your SEP-IRA over your lifetime or over the joint life expectancies of you and a beneficiary.

When you reach age 70$1/2$, you or your employer may continue to contribute to a CODA or a SEP, even though you are no longer eligible to contribute to a regular IRA.

At age 70$1/2$, you must begin to take minimum distributions from all of your retirement plans, including CODAs and SEPs. This means that, in the same year, you could be contributing and withdrawing money!

If you receive a distribution of more than $150,000 annually ($750,000, if the distribution is one lump sum) from retirement plans, you may have to pay a 15 percent penalty tax on the excess. The success penalty is covered in more detail in Chapter 14.

────────────→ **ACTION ITEM** ←────────────

If you are receiving, from all retirement plans, more than $150,000 per year ($750,000, if the distribution is one lump sum), talk to your retirement plan administrator to see whether there are ways to avoid the 15 percent penalty tax.

Can you summarize the primary differences between a SEP-IRA and a CODA-SEP?

A SEP-IRA is a retirement plan set up by your employer, who makes contributions for each employee. The contributions are optional, but your employer may not discriminate.

Contributions cannot exceed the lesser of 15 percent (13.043 percent, for noncorporate employers) of your income or $30,000. If your employer does not contribute up to the IRA limit of $2,000 ($2,250 including a nonworking spouse), you can contribute the difference.

A CODA-SEP is a SEP-IRA retirement plan that allows you to contribute a percentage of your income, through payroll deductions, to the plan. Your contributions cannot exceed $8,728 (in 1992). Your employer may also contribute, as long as the combined contributions do not exceed the lesser of 15 percent (13.043 percent, for noncorporate employers) of your income or $30,000.

What happens if too much money is contributed to my SEP or CODA?

If employer contributions exceed the limits (see the preceding answer) a 6 percent excess contribution tax will be due, unless the excess contribution is withdrawn before you file your income tax return. The same holds true for any excess amount you may have contributed. Contributions withdrawn after the filing of your return may be subject to an additional early distribution penalty.

Income earned on the excess contribution, regardless of when you file your income taxes, may be subject to an early distribution penalty.

What happens to my CODA if I am participating in another retirement plan?

Generally, if you are a participant in another retirement plan, contributions to a CODA are not affected. However, if you are contributing to a tax-sheltered annuity, your combined TSA and CODA contribution is limited to $9,500.

Can I borrow from my CODA or SEP?

SEPs and CODAs do not allow borrowing. If you take money out of these plans, the withdrawal is considered a distribution and will be taxed. If you are younger than 59$\frac{1}{2}$, it will also be subject to an early distribution penalty.

Will contributions to a SEP or CODA affect my social security?

No, they won't. Contributions made by your employer to a SEP or CODA don't count as compensation for social security purposes. Contributions made by you reduce your net income, but they still count as compensation for social security purposes and do not reduce the tax you pay into social security.

If you are more than a 5 percent owner of a business or are considered under IRS rules to be highly compensated, SEPs may be integrated with social security. This means that your SEP and social security could be considered one program. For a broader explanation of social security integration, see Chapter 12.

If I die before distributions begin, how will my SEP or CODA be distributed to my beneficiary?

Distribution of SEPs or CODAs to a beneficiary follows the same rules as IRAs. If you had not been withdrawing funds at the time of your death, your beneficiary may elect not to receive a distribution for up to 5 years. Within these 5 years, beneficiaries other than spouses must receive all inherited funds from the SEP or CODA and pay income taxes on the distribution. If, however, during this 5-year period, the deceased owner would have been age 70$\frac{1}{2}$, distributions to the beneficiary must begin, unless rolled into a spousal IRA.

Additionally, named beneficiaries may elect a lifetime annuity payout, if distributions begin within 1 year of the owner's death.

If your beneficiary is a spouse, an additional option is available. Within 5 years of the date of death of the owner, the spouse may roll the SEP or CODA into his or her own spousal IRA and defer any income and tax until the new owner reaches age 70$\frac{1}{2}$.

If I die after my SEP or CODA distributions have begun, how will the balance be distributed to my beneficiary?

If you were receiving payments from a SEP or CODA according to a payout schedule, your beneficiary, including a spouse, must receive distributions at the same rate or at a faster rate than you had been receiving them.

If an employee is not eligible for a SEP or CODA, what retirement plan options are available?

If you (and your spouse) are not eligible for a SEP or CODA, you quite likely can deduct a regular IRA contribution.

─────── POINTS TO REMEMBER ───────

▸ SEPs and CODAs are particularly appropriate for the small employer.

▸ A SEP is related to a retirement plan and to an IRA. Your employer contributes up to 15 percent of your income to the plan. If your employer's contribution is less than $2,000, you can make up the difference.

▸ The CODA, or CODA-SEP, resembles a 401(k) plan. Qualified employees can contribute a percentage of their income, up to $8,728 (1992), through payroll deductions.

▸ The CODA-SEP may be used only when an employer has 25 or fewer eligible employees and at least 50 percent of these participate in the plan.

▸ SEPs and CODA-SEPs do not allow borrowing.

12

Retirement Plan Payout Options

*U*nderstanding your retirement plan really means understanding exactly what you will receive and how your survivors will fare. Usually, the more income you want at retirement, the less your survivors receive. This chapter covers the many different pension payout options. It shows you how to determine what you and your survivors can expect to receive, and how to adjust your payouts to meet your family's needs.

ESTIMATING RETIREMENT BENEFITS

Under pension rules, your plan administrator may use one of several methods to determine your future retirement benefit. Some of these methods are more complicated than others.

The most common way of estimating a future retirement benefit is to base it on past earnings history and current salary level. Plan administrators use your historic salary trends and build in a growth or inflation rate, to arrive at the "estimate" shown on your benefits statement.

Sometimes, retirement benefits are determined by a complicated system that combines the length of time you have worked for your employer with your earnings *and* your anticipated social security benefits. This is known as an "integrated" plan.

Other administrators may base your benefit solely on the length of time you have worked for your employer, or on your highest income years.

Information on how your retirement benefit is determined and paid out is included in a benefits "booklet" or "packet" given to you when you are hired. The booklet may be just a pamphlet, or, as in government plans, it may be a real encyclopedia!

If you do not know how to determine your benefit or whether it will be integrated with social security, contact the administrator of your plan. You should understand how your plan works, and how benefits accumulate, well before you get ready to retire!

Remember, payout options are usually permanent; you will want to choose the best one when the time comes.

SOCIAL SECURITY INTEGRATION

If your plan is integrated with social security, your employer considers your retirement benefit and your estimated social security payment to be one retirement program. At retirement, however, you will still receive two checks: one from the plan and one from the government.

For example, assume that, at retirement, you will receive $1,000 from a nonintegrated retirement plan and $400 from social security, for a total benefit of $1,400. With an integrated plan, under complex rules, roughly $300 of your social security could offset your retirement plan. Thus, your retirement plan would have to pay you only about $700. You would receive $400 from social security, but total income to you under an integrated plan would be about $1,100—a $300 monthly difference!

WEALTH BUILDING PROFILE

Realizing Too Late. Lila never realized that the pension amount her company always touted was a combined pension and social security payment. The employee benefits booklets mentioned something about integration, but who ever took time to figure out what that really meant? Lila focused on the amount of money she would receive, not how it was arrived at or from what sources.

Lila's words say it all: "I guess I was living in a dream world. I just assumed the $800 was *in addition to* my social security, not *including* it!"

─────────────────→ **ACTION ITEM** ←─────────────────

**Contact your benefits representative and deter-
mine whether your retirement plan is integrated
with social security.**

PAYOUT OPTIONS

A payout option is the method your employer uses to pay out your
retirement benefit. You can choose among different methods, or options. The options can be for a single life (your life only) or joint lives
(yours and a survivor's), or for a certain period of time. Unless otherwise stated, the benefit shown on your statement is almost always a
single life payout option.

THE SINGLE LIFE OPTION

A single life payout option allows you to collect a retirement benefit
for *your entire life*. The benefit starts when you retire and stops at
your death. The single life payout option can be chosen by unmarried
and married people.

THE JOINT AND
SURVIVOR OPTION

Another option usually available is the joint and survivor (J & S)
option. It allows you to receive a retirement benefit during your life
and to guarantee *income to someone else after you have died*. Usually,
the J & S option guarantees income to a spouse, but a single person
often may select a survivor. Under some plans, survivor benefits are
restricted to immediate family members. Two of the most common
J & S options are the joint and 50 percent survivor option, and the
joint and 100 percent survivor option.

The 50 percent option provides to the survivor half of the amount
the employee had been receiving from the pension. The 100 percent
option provides to the survivor a benefit equal to the full amount the
employee had been receiving (see Table 12–1).

Table 12–1
Sample Single Life and Joint and
Survivor Retirement Payouts

	Joint and Survivor[1]	*Survivor Only*[2]
Single life	$500	$ 0
J & S 50%	$400	$200
J & S 100%	$350	$350
10-year certain	$450	$450[3]

[1] Employee's and survivor's retirement benefit.
[2] Survivor's benefit for life (except 10-year certain) if employee dies after retirement.
[3] Survivor's benefit for up to 10 years after employee's retirement date.

Some plans offer additional joint and survivor options, such as 33 1/3 and 66 2/3 percent options. These other options are available only at the discretion of the plan administrator.

THE PERIOD-CERTAIN OPTION

Your plan may guarantee *income for a certain period of time*. With this period-certain option, the retired employee receives a benefit for life, but, at death, the survivor receives income only if the retiree has not lived longer than the period-certain (usually 5, 10, or 20 years from the *date of retirement*). If the retired employee lives longer than the period-certain, the survivor will not receive a benefit after the employee's death. If the retired employee dies before the end of the period-certain, the survivor will receive a benefit for the rest of the period-certain.

Table 12–1 shows examples of the differences between payments to an employee and survivor under various pension payout options.

PROTECTING SURVIVORS

The joint and survivor option allows your survivor, who probably never did any work for your employer, to be protected after you die. Your own retirement payout will be reduced, however, because it must now spread income over two lives. The basic rule is: the more income to your survivor, the less you will receive as the retired employee.

WEALTH BUILDING PROFILE *Understanding Your Benefits Statement.* Albert had been an employee at the same plant for all of his adult life. Now it was time to retire. Both he and his wife, Olga, were looking forward to receiving a monthly retirement check of $650—the amount shown on the annual benefits statement provided by the company. Unfortunately, Albert and Olga did not have a clear understanding of what this retirement figure represented.

When the day came to make a retirement option decision, they took income over both of their lives (joint and survivor option), not just one life (single life option). Their monthly income ended up being $455, instead of the $650 single life benefit shown on the statement.

→ ACTION ITEM ←

If survivor options are not shown on your benefits statement, find out from your benefits representative whether the estimated retirement benefit is for a single life or for joint lives.

You may want to choose the highest benefit possible, especially if you are single. The single life benefit gives you the highest income, but it stops at your death. If you are supporting a relative or want to leave your retirement benefit to someone else, choose a joint and survivor option or (more likely) a period-certain option. Keep in mind that your retirement plan may not allow single people to elect a survivor option.

→ ACTION ITEM ←

If you are single, find out from your benefits representative whether your retirement plan will allow you to sign up for a survivor benefit option.

The period-certain option is the trickiest of all the options. The point most often overlooked regarding this option is that the survivor usually receives income only if the retiree has not lived longer than the period-certain. If the retired employee dies before the end of the period-certain, the survivor will probably only receive a benefit for the rest of the period-certain. The period-certain typically starts at the date of retirement, *not* the date of death.

WEALTH BUILDING PROFILE   *Planning Ahead.* George decided that his ailing wife, Gloria, needed his full-time attention. Doctors told him that Gloria's illness, although not immediately critical, would eventually result in her death. George decided to retire and be with her.

After meeting with the company benefits personnel and thoroughly discussing all the retirement benefit options, George and Gloria decided that a 10-year period-certain option would be their best choice. This option gave them the highest possible current income, while still protecting the survivor.

They assumed that George would outlive Gloria, because she was expected to live no longer than 10 years.

However, in the event George died prematurely, Gloria would be able to receive monthly income for 10 years after the date George retired.

CHOOSING THE BEST OPTION

Choosing the best option means doing a lot of homework regarding your other retirement income sources, family circumstances, health, anticipated life expectancy, and so on. If you are in good health, you may want to combine your pension option with other financial planning techniques, for example, enhancing it with insurance. This pension enhancement method is discussed in Chapter 19.

While you are alive, your spouse or other beneficiary shares your benefit: you receive a joint (family) benefit. If you have retired and you die, the survivor option takes effect: your spouse receives some percentage (usually 50 percent or 100 percent) of your joint benefit.

—————————→ **ACTION ITEM** ←—————————

Create a chart similar to the one below, using *your own* numbers and the options available through your pension plan. You may have to ask your benefits representative to help you fill this out.

	Joint and Survivor	Survivor Only
Single life	$_____	$_____
J & S 50%	$_____	$_____
J & S 100%	$_____	$_____
J & S _____%	$_____	$_____
_____-year period-certain	$_____	$_____

WEALTH BUILDING PROFILE *Silent Only So Long.* Bob's company is changing. He decides to retire now, rather than go through the change. He knows he'll have to make a permanent choice regarding his pension, so he meets with a benefits representative to be sure he understands what to expect. Together, they examine Bob's payout options.

As a married man, Bob has three choices of joint and survivor options: the 50 percent J & S, the 75 percent J & S, and the 100 percent J & S. Given his age, his wife's age, and the pension formula, the choices look like this:

▶ 50 percent J & S: $900 a month to Bob and his wife when he retires. After retirement, if Bob dies first, his wife will start receiving a check for half of that amount, or $450 a month, for as long as she lives. If his wife dies first, Bob will continue to receive $900 a month as long as he lives.

▶ 75 percent J & S: $820 a month to Bob and his wife when he retires. After retirement, if Bob dies first, his wife will start receiving a check for three-fourths of that amount, or $615 a month, for as long as she lives. Bob will continue to receive $820 if his wife dies first.

▶ 100 percent J & S: $760 a month to Bob and his wife when he retires, and the same amount to either of them as long as they live.

Bob asks the benefits representative what he recommends, but gets this answer: "You'd better talk this over with your wife. She's the one who will be affected most. She may end up with $450 a month to live on, or $760 . . . quite a difference."

Bob agrees that his wife *will* have something to say about this!

YOUR LAST CHANCE TO CHOOSE AN OPTION

You can choose either the joint and survivor (50 percent or 100 percent) option or the single life benefit on the day you retire. These are guaranteed options. Some employers require that you put *any other* option on file with the benefits department for a year or more before it can take effect. Therefore, if you want an option other than the guaranteed options, you may have to decide now!

 **ACTION ITEM** ←

Ask your benefits representative these two questions:

▶ **Do you need to have an option on file?**

▶ **How long does an option have to be on file before it becomes effective?**

WHEN YOUR BENEFICIARY DIES BEFORE YOU DO

If you are still working for the company and your spouse or other beneficiary dies, you may simply change your option. Once you have retired, generally speaking, the option you chose at retirement (50 percent or 100 percent option) will be the option you live with for the rest of your life.

A few plans offer an additional option, commonly known as the restore option (covered in Chapter 19). This allows the retired employee to step back into the single life option if the spouse dies first.

───────────────── ➤ ACTION ITEM ◄─────────────────

You will be the retired employee. Find out how your retirement benefits will change if your spouse dies before you do.

PLANNING FOR INFLATION

Once you begin receiving a pension benefit, it usually remains fixed. Some plans occasionally add a cost-of-living adjustment (COLA) to the benefit, but this adjustment is usually optional. A few organizations, most notably the federal government, routinely increase pension benefits through cost-of-living adjustments.

WEALTH *Inflation Concerns.* When Edna retired from teach-
BUILDING ing 10 years ago, her retirement income was about
PROFILE half of her regular salary during the last year she
worked. She worried that this would not be enough income, especially in later years. However, the State Teachers Retirement Plan has built-in annual cost-of-living increases, based on the Consumer Price Index. In addition, the plan administrators have given Edna periodic bonus retirement checks, when the plan's assets have earned more than was originally anticipated. As a result, Edna's retirement income has almost doubled since she retired.

───────────────── ➤ ACTION ITEM ◄─────────────────

Find out whether your pension plan has ever experienced a cost-of-living adjustment (COLA). Is the COLA something you can count on?

A SPECIAL FEATURE: LEVELING

Leveling is a feature offered by only a few pension plans. Some of these plans represent the largest names in industry!

Leveling allows you to receive a higher-than-normal pension payment in the years before receiving social security. In effect, the plan advances payments to you until social security starts.

When you begin receiving social security payments, your pension will be reduced. Thus, by receiving advanced payments in the early years and reduced pension payments when social security begins, your income is leveled.

WEALTH BUILDING PROFILE
Keeping the Good-Life Level. After 25 years as an engineer with a major electronics company, Emmett decided at age 55 that he was ready to retire. Because he was retiring early, his monthly pension was going to be reduced from about $700 at normal retirement to $600.

Emmett figured that if he could retire and hang on financially until he was age 62, he would then receive another $610 a month from social security. At that time, his total monthly income would be $1,210, which would make retirement comfortable.

At his exit interview with the benefits department, Emmett happily learned that, as long as he was willing to take slightly less, his company would, in effect, advance social security payments to him until he was age 62. In his case, the company would pay him $1,000 per month starting at retirement. Then, at age 62, at the start of his $610 social security payments, his pension from the company would be reduced to $390. Thus, at age 62, his income would continue to be level at $1,000; only the sources of the income would be different.

Emmett elected to take the leveling. He chose the steady but slightly lower retirement income, instead of trying to make ends meet until his social security started.

→ **ACTION ITEM** ←

Find out from your benefits representative whether your plan allows leveling.

If you choose leveling, remember that your pension benefit cannot be reduced because of increases in social security. The two benefits work together in the original calculation but are paid quite separately.

NORMAL RETIREMENT AGE

The normal retirement age, under most plans, is 65. Normal retirement, however, may come much earlier than age 65. Pilots over age 60, for example, may not be allowed to fly commercial aircraft; their normal retirement age may be 60! Professional corporations (law offices, medical practices) have tended to treat age 70 as normal retirement. You should know the retirement age stated in your particular plan.

→ ACTION ITEM ←

Consult your benefits packet to determine the normal retirement age for your retirement plan.

Legislation protects workers who continue on the job past normal retirement age, by allowing them to continue to build retirement benefits. For people older than 65, that doesn't mean that other benefits won't change. In particular, there may be changes in life and health insurance.

→ ACTION ITEM ←

If you are going to be working past age 65, understand any changes that may take place in your insurance plans. In particular, review with your benefits representative how Medicare coverage fits into your health insurance plan.

EARLY RETIREMENT

If you retire before normal retirement age, your pension benefits will be reduced—usually a certain percentage for each month or year before normal retirement.

Some retirement plans, however, pay out at a specific age. If you have one of these plans, it doesn't matter whether you have retired—your pension payout will not begin until you reach a certain age (but not later than age 70$\frac{1}{2}$).

DELAYING THE PENSION PAYOUT

You may retire and not need or want your pension immediately. If your plan administrator allows it, you may delay receiving benefits up to age 70½. By delaying any payout from your pension, your account continues to grow, because it earns interest, dividends, or capital gains. Thus, your benefits should be larger when you do receive them; more money will be spread over fewer years.

Taxes will not be owed on your pension's growth and income until you start receiving the payout.

→ **ACTION ITEM** ←

Check with your plan administrator to determine how much your pension payout will increase if you delay receiving it.

WEALTH   *Knowing the System.* Eleanor had been the assistant
BUILDING   to her company's president for over 20 years. Unfortu-
PROFILE   nately, because the business was not doing very well
                 now, pay raises seemed to be far apart. When a job
opportunity came up with a different employer ("an offer I couldn't
refuse"), Eleanor took it.

Her old employer had started a pension plan many years ago, and faithfully contributed to it, on her behalf, each year. She retired fully vested at age 55. Her old employer wanted to know whether she would like to begin receiving a pension payout.

Having just taken a new position with a different company, complete with pay raises, Eleanor didn't need extra income from her old employer's pension. She decided to contact the pension administrator to find out what would happen if she delayed receiving her benefit for 5 years, when, she assumed, she would retire.

To her satisfaction, she was told that, by delaying receipt of her pension to age 60, her checks would be 10 percent more each month!

When she learned this information, she instructed her old employer not to start sending her pension checks until she told them to— probably in 5 years.

Table 12–2
Life Expectancies at Various Ages

Current Age	Life Expectancy (Years Remaining) Male	Female	Current Age	Life Expectancy (Years Remaining) Male	Female
40	34	38	60	18	21
45	30	34	65	14	17
50	25	30	70	11	14
55	21	25	75	8	10

Source: 1980 Commissioners Standard Ordinary Mortality Table (rounded to nearest age).

ESTIMATING LIFE EXPECTANCY

No one knows exactly how long anyone will live. There are, however, ways to estimate average life expectancy, and those averages are the basis for your plan. The life expectancy most retirement plans use is simply the year in which the greatest number of deaths will occur for your age group. Table 12–2 illustrates life expectancy at various ages. *Your* life expectancy may be more or less than the number of years shown.

How accurate are the benefit statement estimates?

If you are close to retirement, your benefits department can give you very specific amounts based on your and your spouse's actual ages. If you are several years away from retirement, the estimate may not be accurate. The plan administrator does not know exactly what your future pay increases will be, or how much the money in the pension trust will earn in the future. For this reason, some administrators show two or three different estimates, giving you a *range* of possibilities.

Determine whether the estimates you receive show a single life or a joint and survivor payout, and whether they include social security.

What if I don't put an option on file?

If you don't put an option on file, federal laws assign a single life option if you are unmarried, or a joint and 50 percent survivor option if you are married.

Is it possible to receive a pension benefit from my employer's plan if I am still employed?

Yes. As long as you have reached the plan's normal retirement age, a pension benefit can be paid out while you continue to work.

Can I give my future pension benefit to someone?

Generally, future benefits can only be transferred to someone else through a specific court decree known as a qualified domestic relations order (QDRO). This order allows the court to give future pension benefits to a spouse, former spouse, child, or dependent. Otherwise, the courts do not generally allow a pension benefit to be assigned or attached. If it is already being paid out, assignment is usually not possible, other than under the terms of the joint and survivor agreement.

**WEALTH
BUILDING
PROFILE**   *When Paying for Advice Pays Off.* Now that she had the qualified domestic relations order (QDRO) and had been awarded just about everything her attorney said she would get, Martha was pleased.

What satisfied Martha the most about the settlement was the judge's issuing an exception to the usual QDRO. This exception allowed her to begin receiving a pension benefit from her ex-husband's plan when *she* reached 55.

Martha's attorney had told her all along that she was entitled to a portion of her ex-husband's retirement benefit. The only issue had been whether the judge would allow her to begin receiving a distribution from the pension *before* her ex-husband retired. Because her ex-husband was a "workaholic," Martha feared he would never retire.

The attorney brought all this out for the judge to consider. The judge even reviewed the pension plan, to determine the earliest retirement age allowed under the plan. That is how he arrived at age 55.

Now Martha's ex-husband can work forever, if he wants. She'll receive her benefit without worrying about it.

I have an option that allows me to receive my pension in a single distribution. How do I evaluate this choice?

This is probably a distribution that falls under the lump-sum distribution rule. You are in a very enviable position: you have more choices than most people do. Because lump-sum distribution is such a large and important topic, we devote all of Chapter 15 to it.

If my spouse dies after I retire, can my own benefit ever be reduced?

Sometimes, when the spouse dies, plans reduce the benefit paid to the retired employee to that of a survivor. This is quite uncommon, but clearly worth checking into!

——————— POINTS TO REMEMBER ———————

▶ Because payout options are usually permanent, it's important to know everything you can about them, well before you are asked to make your payout option choice.

▶ If your retirement plan is integrated with social security, it includes anticipated social security benefits as part of the total retirement payment.

▶ The single life payout option gives you the highest payout. It starts when you retire and stops at your death. It can be chosen by unmarried and married people.

▶ The joint and survivor (J & S) option gives a benefit during your life *and* guarantees income to someone else after you have died. Your payment will not be as high if you choose a joint and survivor option as it will be if you choose a single life payout option.

▶ If you choose the period-certain option, you and your survivor will be guaranteed retirement income for a certain period of time only—usually 5, 10, or 20 years.

▸ If you are single, your retirement plan may not allow your benefit to go to anyone else after your death.

▸ Some payout options may have to be on file for a year before they can take effect.

▸ In certain plans, you may have to have been married for a year before your spouse is eligible to receive a survivor's benefit.

▸ Once you begin receiving a pension benefit, it usually remains fixed.

▸ If you retire before normal retirement, your pension benefits will be reduced. Different plans define normal differently.

▸ Your future pension benefit may be awarded to your spouse, former spouse, child, or dependent only through a specific court decree known as a qualified domestic relations order (QDRO).

13

Getting Money Out of Retirement Plans Your Employer Controls

Knowing the most effective way to get money out of a retirement plan is an important, yet often neglected, aspect of retirement planning. Most often, we are content with the steady, monthly income option (the primary topic of the previous chapter) as the way to receive a distribution. But that's only one way to receive retirement plan income, and it may not be the best way for you.

Choosing which way to receive a distribution from retirement plans isn't simple, and employers don't usually make it easy. In fact, because of the legal issues surrounding the giving of tax and investment advice, most companies carefully avoid making any suggestions. You're left on your own to figure out what to do.

Fortunately, most of the time you have control over your retirement plan choices; with a little help, you should be able to make them work to your advantage. To do this, though, you must understand and compare all of your options.

MINIMUM AGE VERSUS YEARS OF SERVICE

Retirement plans generally have certain requirements as to how old you must be or how long you must work, before you qualify for a retirement plan payout. Just because you are ready to retire, you won't *necessarily* receive a retirement check! Let's look at all the issues.

If your plan is the type that allows a benefit to be paid after you've worked a *certain number of years* for your employer, no matter what your age, then you have no planning problems. You can retire and begin to receive a retirement check. This is called an immediate benefit.

Your plan may, however, require you to wait until a *certain age* to receive your retirement benefit, even if you stop working several years earlier. This is called a deferred benefit. Deferred-benefit plans usually defer payments to no later than age 55 or 60, but they may force you to wait until age 65. This deferred benefit can be a big trap for the unwary.

Don't forget that vesting also plays a part in the amount you receive. Whether you receive a full retirement check or a partial retirement check will depend on your being fully or partially vested.

REDUCTION FOR EARLY RETIREMENT

Another issue applies to those who want to retire early. If your plan allows early retirement—retirement before the plan's normal retirement date—you may receive a check, but it will be for less than the amount you might have expected. Because the money has to stretch out over more years, you will receive a "reduced" benefit.

ONE-TIME LUMP-SUM DISTRIBUTION

It is also possible that, when you retire, your share of the retirement plan will be determined, adjusted for any early retirement, and paid to you as a one-time lump sum. It will be up to you to invest the money for retirement income.

WEALTH BUILDING PROFILE   *Pensions and a Late Marriage.* Rosemary and John recently married. They are making a serious effort to understand their finances, particularly their retirement plans. Rosemary questions whether it would be a mistake to leave her current job if she can find one nearer their new home.

Their research reveals that Rosemary is partially vested in a retirement plan at the insurance agency where she now works. If she works 2 more years, she will be 100 percent vested and can expect to receive a deferred benefit at age 65.

John's circumstances are different. His first job out of school was for a manufacturing firm. He worked there for 12 years before switching to teaching. He has been teaching now for 7 years, and expects to make it his career.

As they review his retirement plans, they discover that John can expect a deferred pension benefit from the manufacturing firm. If he wants, monthly pension income can begin as early as age 60, although there will be a reduction for each year before age 65.

John is fully vested in his teacher's retirement plan. He will have to work as a teacher for at least 20 years, to be able to receive his full retirement benefit (a benefit not reduced for early retirement).

John and Rosemary decide to start a file to keep track of their retirement plans, especially when each can start and how to apply for it!

Rosemary will stick with her insurance company job for another 2 years, in spite of the commute!

———————→ ACTION ITEM ←———————

Dig deep into the rules for your retirement plan. Be sure you can answer these questions about your current job *and* all your past jobs:

▸ **What is the earliest date you can begin receiving a *full* pension?**

▸ **What is the earliest date you can begin receiving any pension?**

▸ **What is the reduction for early retirement?**

▸ **Are you vested in a retirement plan from this job?**

▸ **Will you get a monthly check, or a lump sum, or do you have a choice?**

Be sure to note the specific *department* to contact when you are near retirement. Don't just jot down a name and phone number; people working in that department are likely to change between now and then!

UNDERSTANDING ANNUITIES

We discussed payout options from pensions in the previous chapter. Annuities are another way in which retirement plans pay benefits to their employees. Put simply, an annuity is a type of savings account with an insurance company. When the account matures, it is annuitized, or paid out, usually monthly or annually, to the annuitant (you). The monthly payments usually last several years, over your entire lifetime, or sometimes over your and a survivor's lifetime, depending on which payout option you chose. The annuity payment to you is fixed (it probably won't change), and it is usually guaranteed by the assets of the insurance company.

Employers often use annuities because of their flexibility. With an immediate annuity, your employer's retirement plan transfers a specific sum of money to an insurance company when you retire. The insurance company calculates the amount of the payment, begins making it to you, and takes on the responsibility for all future payments.

The other method, a deferred annuity, lets your employer purchase an annuity each year for you. These deferred annuities all annuitize, and begin paying out to you, when you reach your retirement date. In this method, your employer transfers the responsibility for your retirement, each year, to the insurance company.

Not all payments have to come from the insurance company. Your employer may use a combination plan, with some benefits paid directly out of the pension trust to retired employees each month, and some benefits paid by the insurance company as an annuity. You would receive only one check that combines the amounts from all sources.

---------------→ **ACTION ITEM** ←---------------
Contact your employer to find out where your retirement check will come from: an insurance company annuity or directly from the pension trust. Find out whether your retirement plan has a history of adjusting benefits to help offset inflation.

Annuities (the payments coming from the insurance company) rarely give you a cost-of-living adjustment (COLA). Benefits paid out of the investments of a pension trust may increase as long as the trust continues to perform well. However, these increases are seldom guaranteed. (A notable exception is the built-in COLA for the federal government, most state governments, and the military. The annual COLA in these plans is usually determined by the previous year's inflation rate.)

WEALTH BUILDING PROFILE   ***Staged Income at Retirement.*** Joseph will retire early, at age 60. He's trying to figure out exactly where his income will come from, and how to adjust to the changes. He has four major sources of retirement income: his pension from his current employer, social security, a retirement benefit from a previous employer, and his own savings, including his IRA.

At age 60, Joseph expects an immediate monthly annuity of $445 from his current employer. Starting at age 62, social security will add an estimated $480 per month. At age 65, the deferred annuity from the previous employer will annuitize and add another $220 per month. Meanwhile, if Joseph needs more money, he can take withdrawals from investments or his IRA. Table 13–1 shows how Joseph's income will build, not including his IRA.

Only social security and Joseph's IRA account can adjust for future inflation.

Table 13–1
Joseph's Income

	Age 60	Age 62	Age 65
Income:			
Current Employer	$445 ——————————————→		
Social Security		$480 ——————→	
Previous Employer			$220→
Total Monthly Retirement Income	$445	$925	$1,145

BORROWING FROM THE PLAN

You may be able to borrow limited amounts from your plan while you are working. Your reason must almost always be hardship—a medical emergency, tuition for education, or the purchase of a principal residence—and you must have exhausted all other sources of funds.

If you are allowed to borrow from your retirement plan, you will be charged interest on the money you borrow, usually at a rate slightly less than the rate for a similar loan from a bank. You must pay the money back in equal payments, at least quarterly, and the loan must be repaid within 5 years. A loan used to buy a principal residence may be extended beyond 5 years. Keep in mind that the interest you pay on the borrowed money is usually not deductible from your income taxes.

One exception to this nondeductible rule involves money borrowed to purchase a principal residence. The interest you pay on the money borrowed from the retirement plan may be deductible, if the plan uses the property as the security for the loan. This arrangement can be very complicated, and few administrators will go to this extent. If your administrator does allow it, be sure to get expert tax advice as to how the transaction should be structured.

With any loan, if you leave your job, your employer may demand full and immediate repayment.

WEALTH BUILDING PROFILE   *Getting a Dream House.* "When we drove down the street and saw the house for the first time, we both fell in love with it. And we hadn't even been looking for a new house! They were asking more than we had ever thought about spending, but we determined to come up with the money."

Marilyn and Dave looked at each other and laughed as they told this story. It hadn't been easy to put together the down payment on their dream house, but they had succeeded. One of the keys to their success was the borrowing provision of Dave's retirement plan at work.

Understanding the rules wasn't exactly simple. Because Dave was vested in $40,000 within the plan, he was able to borrow half that amount, or $20,000. And because the money was to be used to help buy their principal residence, they were able to pay it back over 15 years, instead of the normal 5 years required for loans from the plan.

Under the current tax law, because Dave's plan administrator would not take the property as security, Dave and Marilyn can't deduct the interest on the loan. Still, they feel they're paying the interest to themselves, so they don't mind.

TAXES ON MONEY COMING
OUT OF YOUR PLAN

Retirement benefits, not loans, are generally taxed by the IRS; an exception is your own after-tax contributions. Your before-tax contributions will always be taxed by the IRS.

If you receive your benefit as a lump sum, your after-tax contributions will be distributed to you without any tax consequences. The rest of your lump sum, including before-tax contributions, will be taxed according to the lump-sum distribution rules.

If you receive your retirement benefit as a monthly check, the portion representing your own after-tax contribution may be tax-free, but the rest of the check will be taxable. Seek professional tax advice to determine this tax-free portion!

WEALTH   *Anticipating the IRS.* Sylvia retired in January, and
BUILDING   her first retirement check, for $400, has just arrived.
PROFILE   On the advice of her tax preparer, Sylvia decided not
                to have taxes withheld from her check. She will pay
them on a quarterly basis, using the estimated tax payment rules.

Sylvia immediately starts figuring what amount she should be paying to the IRS.

Sylvia has always paid close attention to her taxes, but this year she has something new to consider: only part of her monthly check will be taxable because some of it is a return of after-tax money she contributed years ago.

After studying her retirement statement and the check stub from her first retirement check, and after a quick call to confirm everything with her tax preparer, Sylvia sees that only 87 percent of each check will be taxable.

This number is based on a calculation that includes the total amount of money that was contributed over the years, plus Sylvia's life expectancy.

Sylvia fills in her estimated tax worksheet. Her total retirement plan income will be $4,800, but only 87 percent, or $4,176, will be taxable. She adds the taxable portion of the pension to her other income for the year, and follows the worksheet step-by-step, to figure her estimated tax payment.

She then repeats the process for her state taxes.

At the end of an hour, Sylvia is satisfied that she has her estimated taxes under control. She's satisfied, too, to know that she isn't paying any more tax than she should be.

➤ ACTION ITEM ◄

Check to see whether you are contributing any of your own money to your employer's retirement plan. Are your contributions made before taxes are taken out or after taxes are taken out?

What happens to my retirement plan if I leave work before I retire?

Here's where the new, faster vesting schedules make a difference. Under these schedules, if you have worked for your employer for 5 to 7 years (depending on the plan), you are fully vested. If you have worked fewer years, you may only be partially vested.

The age at which you receive this retirement money depends on whether your plan has an immediate or a deferred payout. When you receive it, it will usually pay out in monthly checks, with the amount based on the payout option you chose. However, some plans distribute all benefits in one check—a lump-sum distribution. Others let you choose between lump sum and an annuity payout. As mentioned before, if you leave your employer and have outstanding loans from your retirement plan, you will be required to repay them in full.

What if I'm only going to get a small benefit; will I still be able to choose a pension payout option?

Probably not. If the total value of the pension is small (less than $3,500), your employer may simply pay you a lump sum.

How do the federal government retirement rules fit into the discussion of leaving my employer?

If you expect to leave your federal government job, review carefully the rules regarding your retirement plan contributions. The Federal Employees Retirement System (FERS) replaced the Civil Service Retirement System (CSRS) in 1987. How your contributions will be treated depends on which retirement system you are under.

What about the money I'm putting into the retirement plan?

In a few plans, most notably government plans, employees contribute to the plan through payroll deductions. At retirement, the employee gets one benefit, but it comes from two sources, the employee's share and the employer's share.

If you are contributing money to this type of retirement plan, your tax planning may be different. Some plans allow before-tax contributions to the retirement plan; others allow after-tax contributions. The amount of taxes you pay when you retire depends on whether your contribution was before or after taxes.

What other taxes do I need to watch out for?

First, watch out for the early distribution penalty on retirement plan payouts received before you are age 55.

Second, watch out for the minimum distribution requirements starting when you reach age 70½. The penalties for not receiving a distribution when you are supposed to can be as high as 50 percent!

Third, you may be stuck with the success penalty tax. This 15 percent penalty is assessed against very large annual distributions from retirement plans—those that exceed $150,000 per year or $750,000 in a lump sum.

In any of these situations, be sure you seek professional tax advice well before you receive the distribution.

Is there any way to avoid paying federal income taxes on my retirement benefits?

The best you can do is postpone taxation by rolling any lump-sum distributions into an IRA. Keep in mind that monthly retirement checks won't receive any special federal tax deferral or special lump-sum tax rates.

What happens to my retirement plan, if I later go back to work for the same employer?

A special opportunity exists if you leave an employer and take a retirement plan distribution with you. If you roll the lump sum into a separate IRA, called a "conduit IRA," you can later roll the money into a new employer's plan. If you go back to work for the same employer, you can redeposit the conduit IRA into the plan. What is the advantage of redepositing the money? You may be eligible for special tax rates on a potential lump-sum distribution. If you leave the money in an IRA, it will always be taxed as ordinary income.

You will lose the chance of redepositing the money, if you mix the distribution with any other, already established IRA. The conduit IRA must remain separate.

What happens to my retirement benefit if I die before I retire?

The vested portion of your benefit goes to your spouse, or sometimes to another named beneficiary. Under current pension rules, there may be delay before the money begins to be distributed, and the spouse or beneficiary may be entitled to only a percentage of what you would have received.

If the payout is in a lump sum, $5,000 of it may not be taxable as income to the beneficiary. In addition, lump-sum distributions may be taxed favorably under the lump-sum distribution rules.

What happens to my benefit if I die after it begins payout?

If you are receiving a monthly check, your spouse or other named beneficiary may continue to receive a benefit, depending on the payout option you chose the day you retired. Your survivors have no ability to change the decision you made when you retired.

———— POINTS TO REMEMBER ————

▶ When you are ready to retire, you will not necessarily receive a retirement check. You may receive an immediate benefit if you've worked the minimum number of years. Your payment will be a deferred benefit if you have to wait until you reach a certain age to begin your retirement payout.

▶ If you take early retirement, your benefit will be reduced.

▶ Your retirement plan may pay you benefits through an annuity purchased from an insurance company.

▶ If you have retirement income from several sources, including social security, it may not all begin at the same time, particularly if you take early retirement.

▶ While you are working, you may be able to borrow from your retirement plan. Loans are usually restricted to half the vested amount in the account, and they must be paid back over 5 years. Interest on loans from retirement plans is not tax-deductible.

▶ If you take out a loan from your retirement plan to purchase a principal residence, interest and payback rules are different.

▶ Monthly retirement checks will be taxable in the year you receive them. If any of the money represents contributions you made yourself, after taxes had already been paid, you won't have to pay taxes on that money again. It is up to you to figure out your tax-free portion. Consult a professional for help!

14

Getting Money Out of IRAs and Other Retirement Plans You Control

*E*ventually, you must take a distribution from your retirement plan. So far, we've looked only at getting money out of retirement plans that are largely out of your control—those that are controlled by your employer. Now, let's look at ways to get money out of the other retirement plans—those that you contribute to and control.

Waiting until you reach age 70½, when withdrawals must begin, may not be the wisest path to follow. This chapter examines the strict rules that must be followed, to avoid excess taxes and penalties for you and your beneficiaries.

TYPES OF RETIREMENT PLANS

Getting money out of retirement plans that you control varies with the type of plan you have. We've talked about each one of them in previous chapters. Here, we'll break them down into two major types, to aid in our discussion: IRA-type and non-IRA-type retirement plans. The rules regarding them are quite different.

IRA-type retirement plans include:

▶ Individual retirement account (IRA; Chapter 7)

▶ Simplified employee pension (SEP; Chapter 11)

▶ Cash or deferred arrangement (CODA; Chapter 11).

Non-IRA-type retirement plans include:

▶ 401(k) (Chapter 6)

▶ Tax-sheltered annuity (TSA; Chapter 8)

▶ Employee stock ownership plan (ESOP; Chapter 9)

▶ Keogh (Chapter 10).

AVOIDING THE EARLY DISTRIBUTION PENALTY

The early distribution penalty is expensive, and there are too many ways around it to warrant paying it. Let's take a look at how it works and how you can avoid paying it.

The penalty for early distribution, set by the federal government, is 10 percent of the amount withdrawn from your retirement plan—in addition to any federal or state taxes or other penalties you might owe.

As an example, let's say you withdraw $1,000 from a 401(k) plan and are subject to the penalty for early distribution. In addition to state and federal income tax, which could amount to over $400, you will pay a $100 penalty—10 percent of the $1,000 distribution.

Your state may charge a penalty for early distribution, too.

Most people avoid the penalty by simply waiting until they are age 59½ before they withdraw money from a retirement plan. At that age, the early distribution penalty no longer applies. But what if waiting until age 59½ is inconvenient?

The Internal Revenue Code provides several other methods for avoiding the early distribution penalty. First, for non-IRA-type plans, you can avoid an early distribution penalty if you are at least age 55, *retire*, and take your distribution.

You may be able to avoid the early distribution penalty even before age 55. To do this, you must be separated from service (not working for the employer with the retirement plan). If you meet that condition and your former employer will pay out the funds, you can either roll the entire amount into an IRA or take the distribution, *at any age*, as a series of payments based on your life expectancy (or your and your beneficiary's life expectancies). This is usually called an annuity pay-out or a lifetime payout.

You also avoid the penalty if you receive a distribution, *at any age*, under a qualified domestic relations order (QDRO) or if you withdraw money for certain medical care expenses.

For IRA-type plans, you can avoid the early distribution penalty, *at any age*, if you elect a payout spread over your entire life or over the joint life expectancy of you and your beneficiary.

Another way to avoid the penalty for IRA-type plans is to elect a payout spread over at least 5 years or until you reach age 59½, whichever is longer. After that, if you did not elect an irrevocable pay-out option, you can increase, lower, or even stop your withdrawals.

Finally, for *all* retirement plans, if you become permanently and totally disabled, or die, you or your beneficiaries will *not* be subject to the early distribution penalty.

OTHER COSTS

In addition to the cost of taxes and penalties, you must be aware of administrative fees paid to the trustee or administrator. There are three basic types: a flat annual fee, an annual fee based on a percent of your retirement plan value, or a combination of both. If your adminis-trator or trustee is not charging a fee, check to see whether you are receiving a competitive rate of return or whether your fee is being taken out of your investment return.

Don't confuse fees to administer your retirement plan with com-missions or loads that may be part of the investment and separate charges.

→ ACTION ITEM ←

Each year, alert your tax preparer to the fees you pay to your IRA trustee or retirement plan admin-istrator. These fees may be tax-deductible.

INCOME TAXES ON WITHDRAWALS

All retirement plan distributions will be taxed, but the tax may be immediate or deferred, at ordinary or special rates. Planning for taxes is one of your major assignments when you consider your retirement income.

The lump-sum special tax treatment is available for all retirement plans except IRA-type plans *and* TSAs. Distributions from IRAs and TSAs will *always* be taxed as ordinary income. If you roll your non-IRA retirement plan into an IRA, you will lose the ability to use lump-sum special tax treatment on that retirement plan.

Don't overlook the possibility that your plan administrator may not require you to withdraw the money the day you retire. Most non-IRA-type retirement plans allow you to leave the money with the plan after you retire.

CONVERTING YOUR RETIREMENT PLAN TO INCOME

Retirement plan rules allow you to invest in a wide variety of investments. The most common are certificates of deposit, annuities, money market funds, mutual funds, bonds, and stocks. These investments typically produce interest, dividends, or capital gains, all of which can be held in the account to continue to compound, or distributed to you as income.

Usually, getting income is a simple matter of submitting the proper paperwork to your plan administrator. You may ask that all investment income be sent to you, or you may elect a specific payout, say $200 a month, which may include both income and principal. It's up to you to decide the amount and timing of your distribution.

→ ACTION ITEM ←

To find out about investment options within your retirement plan and how distributions can be sent to you, check with your plan administrator.

REQUIRED DISTRIBUTIONS AT AGE 70¹/₂

If you don't need to receive income from your retirement plan, you can delay receiving the income up to April 1 in the year *after* you reach age

70½. At that time, the Internal Revenue Service (IRS) requires that a minimum distribution of all contributions plus earnings must begin.

Even though the IRS uses the April 1 date for you to begin a distribution, the value of the account to determine the amount of the first distribution is established on *December 31 of the year before you turn age 70½.*

There are several ways to figure the minimum you must withdraw. All of them are based on a series of payments to be made to you over your life, or over the lives of you and your beneficiary.

To figure out the amount you must withdraw from your IRAs, add the December 31 values of all your IRAs together, and multiply by a withdrawal rate. The IRS furnishes these rates each year. A sample is shown in Table 14–1, which lists the approximate withdrawal rates at selected ages for a single and joint life.

If you want to determine the required withdrawal on your individual IRA, multiply the December 31 value by the single rate. If you want to figure the minimum required withdrawal for both you and your spouse (a joint life), add your IRAs together and multiply by the appropriate combined rate.

Remember that the values in Table 14–1 are approximate. The IRS issues new tables each year.

WEALTH BUILDING PROFILE   *Making the Distribution.* MaryJo became 70½ on June 12, 1991. She has two IRAs. She must begin receiving a distribution by April 1, 1992. On December 31, 1990, her account balances were $10,000 in IRA-1 and $20,000 in IRA-2. MaryJo's brother, age 65, is the beneficiary of IRA-1 and her husband, age 75, is the beneficiary of IRA-2.

MaryJo's required minimum distributions are: from IRA-1, $430 ($10,000 × 4.3%), the joint and survivor amount for MaryJo and her brother; for IRA-2, $1,060 ($20,000 × 5.3%), the joint and survivor amount for MaryJo and her husband.

The distribution that MaryJo must take by April 1, 1992, from either or both IRAs, is $1,490.

If you elect a joint life withdrawal based on someone (spouse or not) considerably younger than yourself, the required distribution

Table 14–1
Retirement Plans That You Control

Age of Owner	Single Rate	Age of Beneficiary or Joint Rate			
		60	**65**	**70**	**75**
70	6.3%	3.8%	4.3%	4.9%	5.3%
75	8.0	4.0	4.6	5.3	6.1
80	10.5	4.1	4.8	5.7	6.7

←Approximate amount to be withdrawn from IRAs→

Approximate minimum withdrawal rates derived from IRS Publication 575, *Pension and Annuity Income*.

will be smaller. However, if there is an age difference of more than 10 years between you and a *nonspousal* beneficiary, distributions will be based on a 10-year age difference.

WEALTH BUILDING PROFILE   *Extending the Benefit.* Max is an unmarried 70-year-old man with $50,000 in an IRA. The federal government requires that he begin withdrawing funds from his IRA this year.

Max has a 50-year-old nephew of whom he is very fond. This nephew is Max's only living relative.

Because the nephew is his heir, Max decides to name the nephew as his joint life beneficiary on the IRA. By doing so, he will keep his IRA distributions down to a minimum and leave more for his nephew. Max doesn't need the money, so it sounds like a great idea.

Researching joint life beneficiaries, Max learns that, even though his nephew is 20 years his junior, for nonspousal joint life beneficiary purposes, his nephew is only 10 years his junior. That means the money will have to come out faster than Max anticipated, but still not as fast as with a single-life IRA.

CALCULATING THE DISTRIBUTION IN SUBSEQUENT YEARS

To calculate your minimum distribution each year, use your remaining account balance and the distribution rate for your current age. This account balance is established on December 31 of the previous tax year. After the first distribution, each subsequent distribution must be made by December 31 of that current tax year. (Don't forget to subtract the first year's distribution, which probably occurred on April 1 or slightly earlier in the current tax year, before calculating the second year's distribution.)

WEALTH   *B.J. Knows IRAs.* B.J. reached 70½ in September
BUILDING   1991. He must begin receiving distributions by April
PROFILE   1, 1992. B.J.'s IRA account balance as of December
                   31, 1990, is $10,000. The required minimum distribu-
tion based on his single life expectancy is $630 ($10,000 × 6.3%). This amount will be distributed to him on April 1, 1992.

By December 31, 1991, B.J.'s IRA account balance is $10,500. To calculate the minimum amount required to be distributed for 1992, the $10,500 is reduced by the $630 minimum required distribution for 1991 (even though it will not be withdrawn until April 1, 1992), and the account balance of $9,870 is used. Because B.J. is now 71, the withdrawal rate for age 71 is used.

PENALTIES FOR UNDERWITHDRAWAL

If you don't withdraw the minimum required each year, the IRS can penalize you *up to 50 percent* of the amount you failed to take out!

→ ACTION ITEM ←

List your IRAs and other retirement plans. If you will be 70½ this year, use IRS Publication 575 to determine your required distribution, or contact a tax professional to help you.

HOW YOUR BENEFICIARY
RECEIVES YOUR IRA

If you had not been withdrawing funds from your IRA (including SEPs and CODAs) at the time of your death, your beneficiary may elect not to receive a distribution for up to 5 years. Within these 5 years, beneficiaries other than spouses must receive all funds from the IRA and pay income taxes on the distribution. If, however, during this 5-year period, the deceased owner would have been age 70½, distributions to the beneficiary must begin, unless rolled into a spousal IRA.

Additionally, named beneficiaries may elect a lifetime annuity payout on their life, if distributions begin within 1 year of the owner's death.

If your beneficiary is a spouse, one additional option is available: within 5 years of the date of death of the owner, the spouse may roll the IRA, tax-free, into a spousal IRA and defer any income and tax until the new owner is age 70½.

Use the decision tree shown in Figure 14–1, to aid you in determining withdrawal options for a deceased owner's IRA, SEP, or CODA.

If you were receiving payments from your IRA, SEP, or CODA according to a payout schedule, your beneficiary, including a spouse, must receive distributions at the same rate or at a faster rate than you had been receiving them.

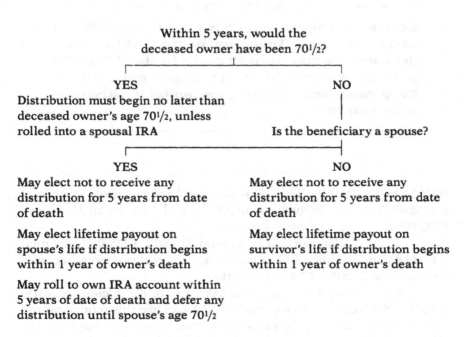

Within 5 years, would the
deceased owner have been 70½?

YES	NO
Distribution must begin no later than deceased owner's age 70½, unless rolled into a spousal IRA	Is the beneficiary a spouse?

YES	NO
May elect not to receive any distribution for 5 years from date of death	May elect not to receive any distribution for 5 years from date of death
May elect lifetime payout on spouse's life if distribution begins within 1 year of owner's death	May elect lifetime payout on survivor's life if distribution begins within 1 year of owner's death
May roll to own IRA account within 5 years of date of death and defer any distribution until spouse's age 70½	

————— Figure 14–1 —————
Beneficiary choices: IRAs, SEPs, and CODAs.

WITHDRAWALS FROM NONDEDUCTIBLE IRAs

Under current tax law, you cannot single out your nondeductible IRA contributions for withdrawal. Nondeductible IRA contributions must be withdrawn at the same rate as your deductible and rollover IRAs. This means that a portion of your IRA will come out tax-free for each year in which you withdraw money from your IRAs.

For example, if your contribution to a nondeductible IRA is $1,000 and you withdraw your IRAs over 20 years, $50 ($1/20$ of $1,000) will be tax-free each year.

Once you begin making nondeductible IRA contributions, you are required to fill out federal Form 8606 each year, until withdrawals are completed. If you fail to file Form 8606 with your tax return or are otherwise unable to prove some of your contributions were nondeductible, all of your nondeductible contributions could be taxed when withdrawn.

─────────────── ➤ **ACTION ITEM** ◄ ───────────────

Keep a copy of each year's federal Form 8606 in a permanent file. When you begin making withdrawals, you may need to prove to the IRS that a portion of your IRA money comes out tax-free. Keep these forms until the last dollar is withdrawn from your IRA.

WEALTH BUILDING PROFILE   *Costly Trip.* Howard has kept accurate records of his deposits to his IRAs and how much they have earned over the years.

His current IRAs total $10,000. $2,000 of this total is from a nondeductible IRA contribution; the rest is interest accumulation and deductible IRA contributions.

Howard is retired and wants to take a trip. He decides to withdraw $2,000 from his nondeductible IRA and use this money for the trip. It is easy for him to identify this money because he has kept it in a bank account totally separate from his other IRAs. He reasons that, because the money that went into this account was not tax-deductible, it should be tax-free when it comes out.

At tax time, his tax preparer has bad news. "You can't simply take money out of a nondeductible IRA and expect it to be tax-free." Howard learns that the IRS treats all IRA accounts as one IRA account, even if a nondeductible IRA account is separate. Thus, the $2,000 he withdrew is a combination taxable and nontaxable IRA.

The calculation looks like this: his total account value was $10,000 and his nondeductible IRA was $2,000. Therefore, 1/5, or $400, of the amount he withdrew will be tax-free, and 4/5, or $1,600, will be taxable.

Howard's trip cost him more than he wanted to spend.

THE "SUCCESS" PENALTY

If you receive a distribution of more than $150,000 per year ($750,000, if the distribution is one lump sum) from an IRA or any other retirement plan, you may have to pay a 15 percent penalty tax on the excess. These distribution amounts are known as the "safe-harbor" threshold. The penalty tax over this safe-harbor amount is known as a "success" penalty. This penalty is added on to any other tax or penalty you may owe as a result of a distribution from a retirement plan. Remember, *all* retirement plan income is combined.

An alternative method of determining when the success penalty begins is the "inflation adjusted" method. This method uses a 1992 figure of $140,276 ($701,380, if the distribution is one lump sum) and adjusts for inflation each year. This alternative inflation adjusted method is not often used, because the safe-harbor amount is much higher. For individuals with large retirement plan accounts, the required minimum withdrawal at age 70½ may trigger this success penalty. For this reason, it may be better to begin withdrawing money before age 70½, to keep withdrawals below the success penalty threshold.

———————→ ACTION ITEM ←———————

If you are receiving, from all retirement plans, more than $150,000 annually ($750,000, if the distribution is one lump sum), ask your retirement plan administrator whether there are ways to receive less income, to avoid the 15 percent penalty tax.

?

If special tax treatment is available, why would I want to roll a retirement distribution into an IRA and have it later taxed as ordinary income?

As a general rule, if you are withdrawing an amount less than $50,000 from a non-IRA-type retirement plan (except a TSA), you will want to use the special tax averaging because of the favorable tax rates. For amounts greater than $50,000, as long as you don't need the money for many years, tax-deferred compounding in an IRA can result in your having more money. (You can take advantage of compounding by leaving the money in the plan, too.)

The primary risk you run by not using the special tax averaging is the possibility of higher tax rates when you finally withdraw the money.

Are future tax law changes a concern?

Yes! Future tax laws may affect retirement plan withdrawals and lump-sum distributions. Many tax professionals recommend using the special tax averaging methods now, while these methods are still available. We can only guess about future tax laws and how they will affect distributions from retirement plans.

If I roll my non-IRA-type retirement plan into an IRA, does that mean I can't receive any income from it?

No. The investments you make within your IRA will probably produce interest income, dividends, or capital gains. These earnings can be distributed to you, although they will be taxed.

If I take only a minimum withdrawal, how long will my retirement plan last?

The rate of return you get on your investments within your retirement plan is a big factor in determining how long it will last. However, if you make withdrawals based on the joint or single life tables and earn a reasonable rate of return on the remaining balance, say 7 or 8 percent, your account will continue to grow for at least 10 years. After that, as you withdraw money, your account balance will decrease. Chapters 18 through 21 show ways to estimate how long your account will take to reach zero.

WEALTH BUILDING PROFILE   *Marianne's Dilemma.* When Jack died, Marianne received a $100,000 lump-sum distribution from his 401(k) plan. As a spouse, she can choose either an IRA rollover or 10-year special averaging. After studying the 10-year averaging rules, she finds that she would pay over $14,000 in federal taxes alone on the distribution! This would leave her with less than $86,000 to invest.

Because of income from insurance proceeds and other sources, she does not expect to need a distribution from principal for several years. However, she might need the interest income that the money earns.

Because Marianne doesn't need the principal now and may need only some of the income later, she decides to roll the full $100,000 into an IRA. While in the IRA, the full $100,000 will grow because of compounding interest. If Marianne wants to receive income from this money, the IRA administrator can make a distribution to her. This distribution will be taxable.

By not taking distributions from her IRA, Marianne can delay paying taxes on this lump-sum distribution for several years. Thus, the tax-deferred compounding will work in her favor.

If I have more than one retirement plan, how do I calculate the minimum withdrawal?

To determine your minimum distribution, you must combine the values of *all IRAs, SEPs, and CODAs* that you have. The minimum payment must include the values of *all* accounts but the required distribution can be taken from *one* account.

If you have any other retirement plan (401(k), TSA, Keogh, or other type), a withdrawal must be made from each. Thus, for withdrawal purposes, *different retirement plans* cannot be combined to calculate the minimum distribution.

——————— POINTS TO REMEMBER ———————

▶ Waiting until age 70½, when you must begin withdrawals, may not be the wisest path to follow. It may lead to an unnecessarily large estate and be taxed excessively at your death.

▶ Early withdrawals are not usually wise, either. The 10 percent penalty for early distribution is expensive and there are too many ways around it to warrant paying it!

▶ For 401(k), TSA, ESOP, and Keogh plans, you can avoid the early distribution penalty if you are at least age 55, *retire*, and take your distribution.

▶ For IRAs, you can avoid the early distribution penalty *at any age* if you elect a payout spread over your entire life or over the joint life expectancy of you and your beneficiary.

▶ For all retirement plans, if you become permanently and totally disabled, or die, you or your beneficiaries will not be subject to the early distribution penalty.

▶ All retirement plan distributions will be taxed, but the tax may be immediate or deferred, and it may be at ordinary or special rates. Tax planning is one of your major assignments, when you consider your retirement income.

▶ IRAs, TSAs, SEPs, and CODA-SEPs are always taxed as ordinary income. Special lump-sum tax treatment is available for all other plans. Lump-sum rates are usually better than ordinary income rates.

▶ As a general rule, if you are withdrawing an amount less than $50,000 from a non-IRA-type retirement plan (except a TSA), you will want to use the special tax averaging rates available to lump-sum distributions.

▶ For amounts larger than $50,000, as long as you don't need the money for many years, rolling the money into an IRA and letting it all grow, tax-deferred, may result in your having more money when you finally withdraw it.

▶ At age 70½, distributions *must begin* from your retirement plans. The amount you must withdraw depends on your life expectancy (and that of your beneficiary, if you wish to use two lives to do the calculation).

▶ All IRAs must be combined when you calculate the amount of the withdrawal, but it may be taken from *one* account.

▶ Nondeductible IRA contributions must be withdrawn at the same rate as your deductible and rollover IRAs.

15

Lump-Sum Distributions

A lump-sum distribution occurs when your entire retirement account is paid to you in one calendar year. The prospect of receiving sudden money can be very exciting, even overwhelming—and very complicated, if you don't need the money just yet. Understanding all your options may take special effort, but you will usually have the opportunity to do proper tax and investment planning around a large distribution only once in your lifetime!

This chapter presents the issues involving a lump-sum distribution. By following through on the Action Items, you'll be confident you are doing the best job possible to correctly handle your distribution.

PLANS QUALIFYING FOR A LUMP-SUM DISTRIBUTION

Do you qualify for lump-sum benefits? Even if *you* do, does your plan qualify? Learning about the applicable rules can be time-consuming, but the long-term financial benefits make it all worthwhile.

First, identify your plan type. Use the worksheet on page 170.

Will your plan distribute all of your accrued benefits in one calendar year? If your plan distribution is spread over more than one tax year, as in the form of an annuity, your distributions will generally be taxed as ordinary income and will *not* be eligible for lump-sum treatment. For plans having end-of-the-year distributions spilling into the following year, the IRS makes allowances.

Wealth Building Worksheet

Check the retirement plan or plans that will yield distribution(s) to you:
_____ 401(k)

_____ TSA (tax-sheltered annuity)

_____ Pension

_____ Profit-sharing

_____ Keogh

_____ IRA (individual retirement account)

_____ SEP (simplified employee pension)

_____ CODA (cash or deferred arrangement)

_____ ESOP (employee stock ownership plan)

Next, from the decision trees in Figure 15–1 and Figure 15–2, determine your tax choices. Note that distributions from IRAs, SEPs, CODAs, or TSAs do not qualify to use special tax treatment.

→ ACTION ITEM ←

- **Check with your benefits representative to determine whether your accrued retirement plan benefit can be distributed to you in one calendar year.**

- **If your retirement plan makes a distribution to you over two calendar years, check with a tax professional to see whether this distribution qualifies for special lump-sum tax treatment.**

YOUR QUALIFICATIONS

To receive the special tax treatment, you must meet certain requirements. If you meet these requirements, you will be able to use a very favorable way of having your lump-sum distribution taxed, under either 10-year or 5-year special averaging tax rates. Let's look at what is involved.

First, you must have been in the plan for at least 5 years and be eligible to retire. Next, to qualify for the best tax treatment, known as

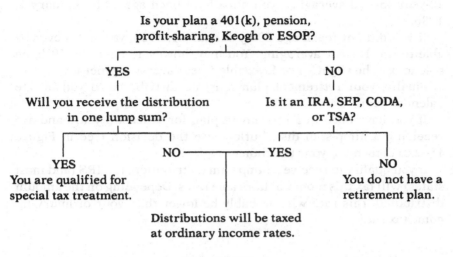

Figure 15–1
Lump-sum eligibility.

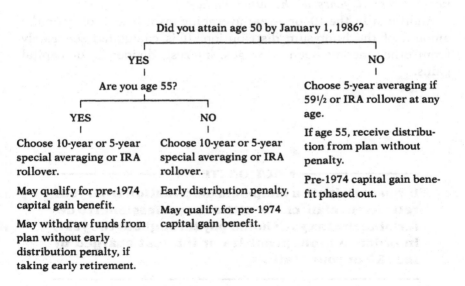

Figure 15–2
Your distribution choices.

10-year special averaging, you must have been age 50 by January 1, 1986.

If you did not reach age 50 by January 1, 1986, you will never be able to use 10-year averaging. You may, however, after age 59¹/₂, be able to use the slightly less favorable 5-year averaging method.

Finally, your retirement plan must be distributed to you in one calendar year.

If you have been in a retirement plan for at least 5 years and are receiving a lump-sum distribution, use the decision tree in Figure 15–2 to determine your tax choices.

If you qualify to receive a lump-sum distribution, the IRS (and most states) will tax this money at favorable rates. Depending on the amount distributed, this rate will probably be lower than your ordinary income tax rate.

10-YEAR AND 5-YEAR SPECIAL AVERAGING TAX METHODS

These terms, 10-year special averaging and 5-year special averaging, sound confusing, but they are simply the names the IRS has given to certain tax rate schedules. This tax is *paid only one time in one year, not over 5 or 10 years, as the name implies.*

Additionally, the 10- or 5-year averaging tax is based solely on the amount of the lump-sum distribution. It is calculated separately from other income such as wages, interest, dividends, or capital gains.

--------------------→ ACTION ITEM ←--------------------

If you anticipate a lump-sum distribution from your retirement plan, check with a tax professional to determine the tax you should pay throughout the year, in order to avoid penalties or interest charged by the IRS or your state.

Table 15-1

Percent of Federal Taxes Owed on Lump-Sum Distributions

Amount of Distribution	10-Year Method	5-Year Method
$ 10,000	5.5%	7.5%
20,000	5.5	7.5
30,000	8.4	11.0
50,000	11.7	13.8
100,000	14.5	16.4
200,000	18.5	22.2
300,000	22.1	25.5
500,000	28.7	28.0

These figures are approximate and do not include any state tax.

Thus, we can define the tax as a one-time separate tax, based on a lump-sum distribution from certain retirement plans.

The tax will vary, depending on the amount of the lump-sum distribution and whether you qualify for 10-year or 5-year rates. Table 15-1 illustrates the approximate percentage of federal taxes owed on the lump-sum distribution in the year of the distribution. To avoid penalties or interest, the tax should be paid through payroll withholding or in quarterly installments in the year of distribution.

TAXES ON
AFTER-TAX CONTRIBUTIONS

You may not owe taxes on the entire retirement plan distribution. Some contributions to the plan may have been "after-tax"—the money you contributed to the retirement plan *after* you had paid taxes on it. This money will come to you tax-free. All *earnings* (interest, dividends, or capital gains), however, will be taxable.

Each year, your benefits statement should show your before-tax and after-tax contributions. When you retire, you should receive a record of your before-tax and after-tax contributions.

→ ACTION ITEM ←

Check your benefits statement to see whether you have any after-tax contributions in your savings or retirement plan. If you do, this amount will come out to you tax-free.

You may want to consider these after-tax contributions to your retirement plan as an emergency reserve; you can usually withdraw them at any time.

TAX RATE CHANGES

The Tax Reform Act of 1986 generally repealed 10-year special averaging and made 5-year special averaging available. This new tax rate changed in 1987; since 1987, the rates have remained the same. Congress, however, could change these rates or even eliminate this favorable tax treatment in future years.

Although the 10-year averaging method has been repealed, it remains available, on a once-in-a-lifetime basis, for people who reached age 50 by January 1, 1986. For them, this is a frozen tax schedule.

AGE 50 BY JANUARY 1, 1986

If you reached age 50 by January 1, 1986, the IRS allows you to use 10-year special averaging anytime. However, because an early distribution penalty is imposed on distributions prior to age 55, you should think of this age as the earliest time when you would use it. Even at age 55, the rules are strict.

The basic rules for using 10-year special averaging are: you must have reached age 50 by January 1, 1986, must be separated from service, and must have been a plan participant for at least 5 years. If you meet all of these requirements, you can use 10-year special averaging *one time* after age 55, and avoid the early distribution penalty.

Alternatively, if you reach age 59½ and continue as an active employee, as long as you have met retirement eligibility requirements, you can receive a lump-sum distribution and use special averaging. If you use the special averaging, future contributions and accruals to your retirement plan would not be eligible for special averaging.

If you weren't age 50 by January 1, 1986, but you meet all of the other requirements, you can use 5-year special averaging after age 59¹/₂, *one time*.

COMBINING DISTRIBUTIONS FROM MORE THAN ONE PLAN

You must lump together all distributions from all plans that come to you in one tax year, in order to use the special averaging method. This prevents you from electing an IRA rollover for one of the lump-sum distributions.

If different plans distribute lump sums to you in different years, you must choose the year in which you will use the one-time-only special averaging method. On the other plans, you may elect to use the IRA rollover or pay ordinary income taxes.

──────────────→ **ACTION ITEM** ←──────────────

List your retirement plans. For each plan, answer these questions:

▶ **Will the funds come out in one lump sum?**

▶ **When will I be eligible to receive the funds?**

▶ **Do I qualify for the 10- or 5-year method?**

Review your figures, and the current regula-tions, with a tax professional. Special averaging is usually not a do-it-yourself calculation.

POSTPONING TAXES ON LUMP-SUM DISTRIBUTIONS

There are two ways of delaying or postponing taxes on lump-sum distributions from retirement plans:

▶ Do not take a distribution in the year you retire. Most plans allow you to leave the money with the plan after retirement. (Remember that the government *requires* you to begin distributions by age 70¹/₂.)

▶ Move or roll the distribution into an IRA, following the IRA roll-over rules. Taxes will be delayed until you begin withdrawing the money.

LEAVING THE MONEY WITH THE PLAN

The primary advantage of leaving your entire distribution with the plan is that you retain the ability to use lump-sum averaging in the future. Another, not so insignificant, advantage is that you may not feel comfortable making investment decisions yourself. By leaving your money with the plan, you can leave the day-to-day investment decisions to the trustees.

Be careful, though. Don't assume you can leave the lump sum with the plan. Some plans do not allow it.

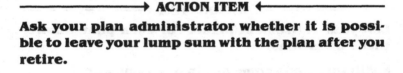

———————▶ ACTION ITEM ◀———————

Ask your plan administrator whether it is possible to leave your lump sum with the plan after you retire.

There may be disadvantages to leaving the money with the plan. The administrator may restrict you by limiting the number of withdrawals you make, or by requiring you to withdraw your money in equal payments over a certain time period, if you don't withdraw it all at retirement.

Your investment choices will be restricted to those within the plan, which may not suit your current needs.

———————▶ ACTION ITEM ◀———————

Check with your plan administrator, to determine the withdrawal and investment limitations you face if your lump sum stays with the plan after retirement.

If you die, your beneficiary may be able to leave your account with the plan, but this is totally up to the plan administrator. Most administrators allow spouses of deceased employees to leave the account with the plan for a certain period of time. When your account is distributed to your beneficiary, $5,000 may be excluded from taxes.

If you withdraw pretax contributions from a plan at any time, other than in a lump sum, they will be taxed as ordinary income. Furthermore, because you have received a "partial" withdrawal, you will no longer be able to use the lump-sum special tax treatment on the remaining amount. (This is true even if you are still working.)

To receive special tax treatment, you must withdraw your money in one lump sum; no partial withdrawals are allowed. The IRS treats partial withdrawals (other than your after-tax contributions) as ordinary income.

WEALTH BUILDING PROFILE   *One More Option.* Roger is planning to retire within the year, but he is worried about how to deal with his savings plan. He can't decide whether to withdraw the money in one lump sum and invest it, or withdraw it and roll it over into an IRA and invest it. His problem isn't so much how to deal with taxes, but how to make the investment decisions.

Until now, Roger's luck with investments has been poor. He isn't looking forward to putting his retirement security on the line.

With this on his mind, he decides to see his benefits representative, to find out whether there are other options.

The representative is quick to point out the one option Roger hadn't considered—leaving the account with the plan and letting the money managers make the investments. When he begins withdrawing the money, they can set up an even payment schedule to last over a certain period of time, for example, $500 a month for 20 years. At the time of his death, any undistributed amount will go to his heirs.

Roger is reminded by his tax preparer that, once a distribution begins, he will no longer be eligible for a lump-sum distribution.

After careful thought, Roger decides to take the income on a monthly basis and let the money managers continue to make the investments. He thinks they will do a much better job than he would.

Don't confuse withdrawals with borrowing. Many retirement plans allow you to borrow (and repay) with little or no tax consequences. However, some plans do not allow borrowing at all. Read the chapter that covers your type of retirement plan, to find out whether borrowing is allowed.

?

If I need income right after I retire, is special averaging the best way to go?

If your retirement plan has options to distribute income to you over a period of years (usually called annuities or payout options), consider those first. Next, compare that income with the income you can receive if you invest an after-tax lump-sum distribution. Often, the annuity or payout option will give you more income. Keep in mind that annuity or payout options are usually irrevocable, once started. Your annuity or payout option won't change to meet changes in your circumstances.

By using another option, the IRA rollover, you may be able to defer the tax liability, invest the money, receive as much income as the annuity or payout option, *and* have investment control!

How will special averaging work if I receive a lump-sum distribution of stock instead of cash?

If your employer's plan allows you to take your distribution in stock, or partially in stock, you have a choice to make. You can choose the special tax treatment on the full value of the stock, or you can pay the tax on your employer's original cost only. Any amount above this cost will be tax-deferred until you sell the stock.

If I decide to use the special tax treatment, will I be subject to the early distribution penalty?

If you qualify for special averaging and you are younger than age 55, you will be subject to the early distribution penalty. However, if you are 55 or older, there will be no penalty, so long as your lump-sum distribution is a result of your retiring.

Remember to investigate your state's requirements, too.

─────────────── ➤ ACTION ITEM ◄ ───────────────

If you receive a lump-sum distribution of stock and want to use special averaging, be sure you decide between:

▶ **Paying taxes now on the full value of the stock, or**

▶ **Paying taxes now on what your employer paid for it, and deferring the rest of the taxes.**

Is special averaging available to the spouse of a deceased employee?

Yes. A spouse receiving a lump-sum distribution from a 401(k), pension, profit-sharing, Keogh, or ESOP plan because of the employee's death is eligible for special tax treatment, if the employee would have otherwise been eligible. This holds true even if the employee was not a participant in the plan for 5 years.

Depending on the plan I have, are my only choices to be taxed at special tax rates or at ordinary income tax rates?

No. One other provision allows retirement plan participants who had capital gains occurring in their plan before 1974 to have these capital gains treated at a 20 percent tax rate. The remainder will be taxed at either the 5- or 10-year special averaging rate.

If you did not reach age 50 by January 1, 1986, this favorable capital gains treatment has been phased out and is not available after 1991.

What happens to special averaging, if I go back to work for my previous employer part-time?

If you are younger than age 59½ and go back to work within one year for the *same company*, you may not be able to use the special tax treatment. You can, however, use the special tax treatment and go to work for *another* employer.

If you are older than age 59½, you can use the special averaging methods and go back to work, at any time, for a new or previous employer.

If you are planning to go back to work for a former employer or a subsidiary of a former employer, on a full-time, part-time, independent contractor, or job-shop basis, consult a tax professional. You may find that you'll be prohibited from using special averaging on a lump-sum distribution you may have received.

Does the success penalty apply to lump-sum distributions?

If you receive a distribution of more than $750,000 in one lump sum from any retirement plan, you may have to pay a 15 percent penalty tax on the excess. Remember, distributions from *all* retirement plans are combined. The success penalty is covered in greater detail in Chapter 14.

If you are receiving $750,000 from all retirement plans in one year, consult a tax professional to see whether there is a way to avoid the 15 percent penalty tax.

Are federal government employees eligible for lump-sum distributions?

At retirement, some federal government employees may choose to take out a portion of their retirement. This distribution may be a return of their own contributions and is not eligible for special averaging treatment or IRA rollover.

------------------ **POINTS TO REMEMBER** ------------------

▶ To be eligible for a lump-sum distribution, your payment must be made to you from a 401(k), pension, profit-sharing, Keogh, or ESOP plan. The payment must represent the entire value of the account, and it must be made during one calendar year. In addition, you must have been in the plan for at least 5 years and be eligible to retire. You are eligible for only one lump-sum distribution.

▶ If you reached age 50 by January 1, 1986, you are eligible for special 10-year averaging; otherwise, you will be eligible for 5-year averaging.

▶ Both the 10-year and the 5-year tax are paid only one time, in one year, not over 10 or 5 years, as the name implies.

▶ If you made after-tax contributions to your plan, this amount will not be included in the lump-sum tax calculation.

▶ If you qualify for special averaging and you are younger than age 55, you will be subject to the early distribution penalty.

▶ There are two ways to delay taxes on lump-sum distributions: postpone taking the distribution, or roll the money immediately into an IRA. Not all plan administrators allow you to leave the money with the plan after you retire.

▶ If you take some money out of your plan, you will have received a partial withdrawal and will be prohibited from using the lump-sum special tax treatment on the remaining amount. *This applies to any withdrawal you may make, even if you are still working.*

16

IRA Rollovers and Trustee-to-Trustee Transfers

*O*ne of the most popular, easy-to-use, and useful tools available in retirement planning is the IRA rollover. It is a way for you to postpone taxes on retirement plans and still manage your own retirement income.

This chapter looks at how the IRA rollover works and at its advantages and disadvantages. Whether an IRA is right for you depends, in part, on when you will need income from your retirement plan.

The basic objective of the IRA rollover is to allow you to move money from one retirement plan to another retirement plan without paying taxes. To accomplish this, as you might expect, you must play by the rules; if you don't, you'll be taxed. Fortunately, the rules are easy to learn and use.

ROLLOVER RULES

An IRA rollover is one of two ways for you to postpone taxes due on a distribution from a retirement plan. One way, as we have previously discussed, is to leave the money with the retirement plan, taking a distribution only when you need income.

Under the rollover rule, you actually receive a distribution (usually a check; sometimes, stock), but you avoid taxes by depositing the proper amount into an IRA within a specific time period.

Not all distributions from retirement plans qualify for an IRA rollover. Those that don't qualify are primarily those distributions that you receive as a series of payments, usually under the annuity or payout option. A distribution of less than one-half the value of your retirement account (a partial distribution) is also ineligible for an IRA rollover.

You may find yourself protesting, "But I can't contribute to an IRA." *Everyone* is eligible for an IRA rollover! Even though you may not currently be allowed to deduct an IRA ($2,000 or $2,250) from your yearly income taxes, you can still roll over your retirement plan distribution, and there are no limits on the amount. You can deposit the distribution into a previously established IRA or establish a new IRA.

ESTABLISHING AN IRA

To do the IRA rollover, you must establish an IRA account. You may already have one, or you may open a new account. The most common places to establish an IRA are at a bank, savings and loan, credit union, insurance company, stock brokerage firm, or mutual fund.

You need not roll your distribution into a single IRA. IRA accounts may be placed with many financial institutions, or you may have several accounts with the same financial institution.

In any case, IRA rollovers must be completed within a certain time period, and there are limits as to how often you can roll over the money.

TIME LIMIT

An easily overlooked, or sometimes misused, rule deals with the amount of time you have to roll your retirement plan distribution into an IRA. It's not unlimited; the rollover must be accomplished within 60 calendar days of the date of distribution.

The date of distribution is usually the date on the check.

When you receive your check, you may endorse it over to your IRA. Or you may spend, invest, or otherwise use the money as you see fit, as long as you deposit the amount you received into an IRA within the 60-day limit.

Remember, the time limit is 60 days, not *2 months*, which may have 61 days.

MISSING THE DEADLINE

If 60 calendar days go by and you haven't rolled your distribution into an IRA, your money will become taxable. If you are in the habit of procrastinating, don't forget that the 60th day may fall on a Sunday or holiday, when financial institutions are closed. Unfortunately, you won't get an extra day!

Don't be lulled into thinking that you can get around the rule because you put your rollover check into the mail before the 60 days are up. The financial institution must *receive* the funds and establish the account by the 60th day. A postmark within the time limit doesn't satisfy the rule.

⟶ **ACTION ITEM** ⟵

If you are planning an IRA rollover, investigate IRA investment options well in advance of the distribution, to be sure you can complete the rollover within the 60 days allowed.

ROLLING STOCKS, BONDS, OR COMBINATION DISTRIBUTIONS

If you receive securities (stocks or bonds) rather than a check, you may deposit these securities into your IRA *if* your IRA administrator allows stocks or bonds in the account. Alternatively, you can sell the securities through a broker and deposit all the money, including any gain, into your IRA. Again, this must be done within 60 days of the date of distribution of the securities.

WEALTH BUILDING PROFILE *Knowing What Can Be Rolled.* Fred received a lump-sum distribution of $20,000 in stocks and $5,000 in cash from his employer's retirement plan. Fifty-five days later, he sold the stock for $22,000. Can he roll over $27,000 ($22,000 from the stock and $5,000 cash) into his IRA?

Fred consults with his tax adviser and discovers, to his surprise, that he can include the $2,000 gain from the sale of the stock as part of his rollover. However, interest he has earned on the $5,000 during the 55 days cannot be rolled into his IRA. This interest will be taxable to Fred.

———————————

You cannot substitute your own money for securities you have received from a retirement plan distribution. To avoid taxes, either the security has to be rolled into an IRA or the security has to be sold and the proceeds rolled into an IRA.

———————————

WEALTH   ***Almost Trapped.*** Rhonda received a distribution of
BUILDING $10,000 in cash and $3,000 in stock, from her retire-
PROFILE   ment plan. She liked the stock and did not want to
sell it.

When Rhonda wanted to roll it into her IRA, she found out that her new IRA administrator did not allow stock in IRA accounts. After thinking about her problem, Rhonda reasoned that, if she now owned the stock, why not put an equivalent amount of cash into the IRA? In other words, she intended to keep the stock and roll over $13,000 cash.

Unfortunately, after checking with her tax preparer, Rhonda learned that the IRA would tax her on $3,000. The tax preparer told her that she had to either roll the stock into the IRA or turn it into cash by selling it, and then roll over the proceeds.

Rhonda decided the tax bite would be too great if she didn't roll the stock into an IRA, so she sold it and rolled over the proceeds.

———————————

——————→ **ACTION ITEM** ←——————
**Check with your plan administrator to determine
whether you will be receiving your distribution as
a check or as securities (stocks or bonds) from
your retirement plan. If you want to roll securities
into an IRA, you must find an IRA administrator
who is willing to accept them.**

THE ONCE-A-YEAR RULE

Once you have rolled your retirement plan distribution into an IRA, you may, at a later date, decide to move it to another IRA. Common reasons are: high IRA administrative fees, or dissatisfaction with investment results.

The IRA rollover rules allow the move, but within limits. The basic rule allows you to move from one IRA to another IRA once every 12 months, *not* once per calendar year. Rolling any portion of the IRA more often than at this interval will cause it to be taxed as though you had received a distribution.

Each IRA account may be rolled over once every 12 months.

EXCEPTIONS TO THE ONCE-A-YEAR RULE

There are exceptions to this rule. Transferring directly between IRA trustees is allowed as often as you like. The distribution cannot go through you, but must instead go directly to another trustee. This is the trustee-to-trustee transfer we referred to in earlier chapters.

If you move the initial distribution from a retirement plan into an IRA, you do not have to leave it there for 12 months before it can be rolled into another IRA. You get one "free" move.

━━━━━━━━━━→ ACTION ITEM ←━━━━━━━━━

If you want to move from one IRA to another IRA more than once every 12 months, use a trustee-to-trustee transfer.

?

Is there a disadvantage to an IRA rollover?

Yes. When you withdraw money, it will always be taxed at ordinary income tax rates. By using an IRA rollover, you give up your ability to use special tax averaging.

Is there a limit on how much I can roll into an IRA?

You can roll a distribution of any amount, as long as it is not considered a partial distribution (less than 50 percent of your retirement plan).

Can I use an IRA rollover if I am still working?

If your retirement plan allows a distribution while you are still working, you can use the IRA rollover. This advantage principally applies to those wanting to expand or diversify their investments.

What happens if I only roll over part of my retirement plan distribution?

As long as your distribution is at least 50 percent of the total account value, you can roll it into an IRA (even if you are still working). However, any amount not rolled over will be taxed as ordinary income when withdrawn from the retirement plan. In other words, if you roll part of your retirement plan distribution into an IRA, you will not be able to use special tax averaging on the money left in your retirement plan.

➤ **ACTION ITEM** ◄

Before you receive a partial distribution from a retirement plan, consider the tax effects of your decision.

If I deposit my retirement plan distribution check into a savings account for 59 days and roll it into an IRA the next day, do I also roll the accumulated interest in the savings account into the IRA?

No. The accumulated interest or dividends, from the time the distribution was made to you to the time you rolled it into an IRA, cannot be rolled into an IRA. However, any capital gain made during this time period can be rolled into the IRA.

Is there any reason I should keep an IRA rollover from a retirement plan separate from my other IRAs?

Yes. If, at a later date, you want to merge this distribution with another retirement plan, the distribution must be held in a separate IRA, not with other IRAs. This type of separate IRA is a "conduit" IRA. If you are not planning to merge your retirement plan distribution with another retirement plan, there is no need to keep it in a separate conduit IRA.

The advantage of the conduit IRA is that, by merging the monies in a retirement plan that is not an IRA, you may regain the ability to use special tax averaging when you eventually take the distribution.

At the end of the year, my employer is going to no-tify the IRS that I received a retirement plan distri-bution. If I rolled the money into an IRA to avoid taxes, what happens?

Your employer must notify the IRS that you have received a distribution from your retirement plan. The IRS will want to tax it. To avoid taxes, you must make the proper entry on your tax return, telling the IRS you have rolled the distribution into an IRA.

───────────────→ **ACTION ITEM** ←───────────────
Keep records of your IRA rollovers in a permanent file. The IRS may want to see these records when you begin withdrawing money from your IRA, which may be years later.

Is an IRA rollover available to my spouse or an-other beneficiary if I die?

If your spouse receives a distribution from your retirement plan as a result of your death, the proceeds may be rolled into an IRA if completed within the 60-day period.

Beneficiaries other than a spouse, however, are not al-lowed to roll retirement plan distributions into an IRA.

Instead, the distribution to them will be taxed as ordinary income. Remember that, if the distribution is made as a lump sum, your beneficiary may exclude the first $5,000 from taxation.

─────── POINTS TO REMEMBER ───────

▶ Not all retirement plan distributions are eligible for rollover into an IRA.

▶ There are no limits on the amount you may *roll over*, although there may be restrictions on how much you can *contribute* to an IRA.

▶ Your rollover need not go into one IRA.

▶ The rollover must be accomplished within 60 days of the date of distribution. The money you redeposit into an IRA need not be the *same* money that was distributed to you, as long as the amount is the same.

▶ If you receive a distribution of stock, you may roll the stock or sell it and roll the proceeds of the sale. In this case, the amount you roll over may not be the same as the amount that was distributed.

▶ Each IRA account may be rolled over once every 12 months, not once every calendar year. There are no restrictions on the number of trustee-to-trustee transfers you can make in a year.

▶ If you receive a distribution from your employer and roll it into an IRA, you must be prepared to prove to the IRS what you did with the money. If you do not prove the fact of the rollover, you will be taxed on the distribution.

17

Making Sure Your Spouse Gets Your Retirement Benefits

*H*ow quickly and correctly would you be able to answer these questions:

▶ If you die while employed, will your spouse receive any of your retirement benefit?
▶ If so, do you know how much the benefit will be?
▶ When it will start?
▶ How long it will last?
▶ Does your spouse know the answers to these questions, too?

Only some retirement plans protect a spouse, if the worker dies while still employed. With other retirement plans, you must be covered by a special benefit, the qualified preretirement survivor annuity (QPSA), for your spouse to receive any of your retirement. (Some plans call this benefit a preretirement spouse option, or preretirement spouse protection. Your employer may call it something slightly different.)

This chapter gives you answers to questions about the QPSA. You'll also learn whether this spousal protection plan is a good deal, or whether you have one at all!

KNOWING WHETHER YOU ARE COVERED

If your company is using a QPSA to protect spouses, you usually can find it on your benefits statement as part of your Survivors' Benefits. Most employers provide the QPSA, at their expense, as part of an over-all benefits package. Some employers, however, make the QPSA available to employees but do not pay for it. In that case, married couples who think the benefit is a good idea must pay for it themselves.

The most common type of pension plan covered by a QPSA is the defined-benefit plan, which guarantees a certain amount of income to you based on your salary, years of service, and so on. Under the QPSA, your surviving spouse gets a percentage of your retirement income. Other plans, such as profit-sharing or money-purchase plans, typically make QPSAs available, but they offer a lump-sum distribution instead of a monthly income.

You may be covered by a QPSA and not know it, especially if the QPSA is being paid for by your employer. If you are *not* covered, how-ever, you probably *will* know about it, because you and your spouse must sign a form to decline the coverage.

WAIVING THE BENEFIT

Some people sign the form to waive the QPSA benefit, thinking it gives the retired employee a higher living benefit (which it does) while still protecting the spouse in the event of the employee's death (which it does not). Don't be misled by poor explanations or badly designed forms. If you *elect out* of participating in the QPSA, your spouse *will receive nothing* from your retirement if you die while still employed!

PAYING FOR THE QPSA

QPSAs are an expensive benefit. Employers must decide whether they want to absorb this cost or pass the cost on to the employees. Both methods are perfectly acceptable; the decision usually hinges on the effort required to "educate" employees on the QPSA.

If the QPSA is entirely employer-paid, the employer can require all employees to participate. This leaves little room for decision on the part of the employees, but makes the program simple to administer.

If the employees are required to pay for their own QPSAs, they must first understand the advantages and disadvantages of the program. In many cases, the complex planning issues are outside the scope of the benefits department. Given this situation, it is no wonder that some companies simply elect to pay for the benefit, avoiding the problem altogether.

A QPSA can be paid for in three ways:

▶ Your employer can pay.

▶ You can pay through payroll deductions.

▶ You or your survivor can pay at retirement by taking a reduction in retirement plan benefits.

If you are paying for the QPSA through payroll deductions, you probably have noticed that the cost goes up each year. This is caused by two factors: your future retirement benefit is increasing each year, and, because you are getting older, the risk of your dying goes up. The QPSA cost reflects these increases.

———————————▶ ACTION ITEM ◀———————————

Determine from your benefits representative how your QPSA is being paid.

If you are using the payroll deduction method to purchase the QPSA, at retirement you may receive a portion of your retirement benefit tax-free. This is a return of the money you paid into the QPSA. It is returned to you, untaxed, over your life expectancy.

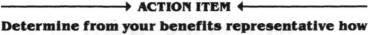

WEALTH BUILDING PROFILE   *Tax-Free Income.* At retirement, Linda had paid a total of $2,000 into the preretirement spousal annuity, through payroll deductions. Her pension was $10,000 a year, and she had a life expectancy of 20 years.

Linda's accountant was well versed in retirement plans. He knew Linda had used a payroll deduction method to pay for her QPSA, and a small portion of her retirement benefit would be tax-free.

He calculated that this annual tax-free portion was $100 ($2,000/20 years = $100). Thus, Linda paid tax on $9,900 for that year.

—————————→ **ACTION ITEM** ←—————————

If you have paid for the QPSA through payroll deductions, take two actions when you retire:

▸ **Determine from your benefits department the amount you paid into the QPSA;**

▸ **Remind your tax preparer that a portion of your retirement benefit will be tax-free.**

QPSA VERSUS INSURANCE

Once you determine your monthly cost for the QPSA, you'll be able to determine, with a little investigative work, whether the cost is in line with the benefit. The easiest way to do this is to compare the QPSA cost with a life insurance policy. Let's go through the comparison step-by-step.

First, find out (from your benefits statement or benefits department) exactly how much your spouse will receive if you die while employed. Next, compare the cost of purchasing an amount of insurance which, when invested, will produce income equal to the QPSA benefit. (You will probably need to work with a skilled insurance agent on this). Finally, determine (from your company benefits booklet) when your spouse would be able to begin receiving the QPSA benefit. With this information, compare the cost of your QPSA with that of private insurance, to determine the better deal.

WEALTH BUILDING PROFILE   *When Research Pays Off.* Max and his wife weren't sure whether the QPSA, that Max was paying for each month through payroll deductions, was a good deal. They had a nagging feeling that the cost was out of line with the benefit, and decided to do some checking around.

Max knew that, if he died before retirement, his wife would not receive anything unless he signed up for QPSA or, alternatively, bought a life insurance policy on his life. If he died while covered by the QPSA, his wife would receive $500 per month for the rest of her life. His wife was healthy but they surmised she would probably not live longer than 30 years, well beyond her normal life expectancy.

If they bought insurance instead of the QPSA benefit, the question was: how much money, in a lump sum, would it take to generate $500 per month for 30 years at a conservative interest rate?

To find this answer, they asked for help from a trusted insurance agent. The agent showed them that, if they could earn 6 percent on their money, a life insurance policy for $85,000 would work.

─────────────────→ **ACTION ITEM** ←─────────────────

▶ **Determine, for each year until you retire, what the QPSA benefit and cost will be.**

Year of Coverage	Amount of QPSA Benefit	QPSA[1] Cost	Insurance Need	Insurance[2] Cost
1992	_____	_____	_____	_____
1993	_____	_____	_____	_____
1994	_____	_____	_____	_____
1995	_____	_____	_____	_____
1996	_____	_____	_____	_____

[1] From your benefits representative.
[2] From a qualified insurance agent.

▶ **Using the life expectancy table in Table 12–2, determine the life expectancy of your spouse. Assuming you can earn 6 percent interest, turn to Table 19–2 and determine the amount of insurance you would need, to equal the QPSA benefit each year.**

▶ **Contact a qualified insurance agent to help determine what your insurance costs would be, to satisfy your need.**

Then they compared prices. The policy would cost less than the QPSA and would return a cash value if Max didn't die before retirement.

Max and his wife bought the policy and canceled the QPSA coverage. They were glad they had spent some time looking into preretirement protection. "It got rid of our worries and saved us a lot of money!"

Insurance is very competitive. It can be less expensive and more flexible than the QPSA benefit, but don't overlook the QPSA advantages. You may be covered by the QPSA even though you cannot pass an insurance medical examination. Coverage is usually guaranteed, and your survivor can't spend it all at once!

→ ACTION ITEM ←

Before you make any decision to drop or not sign up for the QPSA benefit, be sure you are medically able to qualify for insurance.

If I have the QPSA and I die prior to retiring, what will my surviving spouse receive?

Without any other option on file, at your death, your spouse is usually assigned the 50 percent option and receives 50 percent of your vested retirement. Remember, if you have only worked a few years, your vested amount may be very small.

For your spouse to receive anything other than the 50 percent option, you must put an additional option on file with your benefits department. Some plans may not offer you any other choice; others may require you to have an option on file for a period of time before it becomes effective.

When will my surviving spouse receive this money?

Generally, your spouse will not be qualified to begin receiving the QPSA until *you would have* reached retirement age. For some companies, this is 10 years of service; for others, it is age 55. Be sure you and your spouse *both* know when your spouse will receive your retirement income, if you die before retirement.

If you aren't qualified to retire, and you die, your spouse may be in a "blackout" period and will not receive income from your pension for some time.

Could you explain further what "blackout" means?

A "blackout" is a period of time between your death and the date your survivor's benefit begins. For most plans, a survivor's benefit will not begin until you would have been qualified to retire. This could be several years, if you die at a young age.

WEALTH   *What You Don't Know . . . .* Alfred was 56 and
BUILDING   worked for a major aerospace company. At age 55, he
PROFILE   became qualified for retirement, but because early
                     retirement would have caused his income to drop too
far, he decided to continue to work to age 62. Unfortunately, Alfred was overweight and smoked, and he died of a heart attack before he reached his planned retirement.

Alfred hadn't paid much attention to company benefits bulletins. He probably didn't know that, at his death, because the company had previously bought a QPSA for him, his wife, Angela, received a 50 percent survivor annuity. This annuity gave her 50 percent of the monthly pension Alfred would have received at that point. She greatly appreciated it!

Unfortunately, if Alfred had paid a little more attention, he would have found that his company offered options other than the automatic 50 percent spousal benefit. One of the other options Alfred could have chosen was a 100 percent survivor option. This option would have given Angela the full amount of the monthly pension Alfred would have received.

Alfred never read the bulletins, and never filed the form. Angela is receiving a benefit, but she could have received much more!

→ ACTION ITEM ←

▸ **Determine your current retirement benefit from your benefits statement or the benefits department. (This is your vested benefit if you were to die today.)**

▸ **Check with your benefits representative to determine whether you have a QPSA option on file.**

▸ **Ask the benefits representative whether other options are available, and how long these options must be on file to become effective.**

WEALTH BUILDING PROFILE   *Expect the Unexpected.* Bob was well into his career at age 47. He had been with the company long enough to be fully vested in his pension. The year before, he had felt his family needed added protection, so he had signed up for the QPSA.

When Bob was killed in an accident, a company benefits representative met with his widow to let her know that she would receive a survivor's retirement benefit. Unfortunately, only survivors of employees qualified to retire could receive immediate retirement benefits. Because Bob would not have been qualified to retire until age 55, his widow's retirement benefit won't begin for 8 years.

→ ACTION ITEM ←

Understand your employer's preretirement policy. Be sure you can answer this question: If I die before I retire, how much of my pension will my spouse receive, and when will the payments begin?

How long must I be married before my spouse receives the QPSA?

Generally, for your spouse to receive the QPSA, you must have been married at least 1 year before your death. Some plans, however, have no time requirement.

―――――――――→ ACTION ITEM ←―――――――――

If you are newly married, check with your benefits representative to determine when you can qualify for the QPSA.

―――――――――――――――――――――――――――

What if I choose not to use the preretirement benefit?

If you choose not to use the QPSA, your spouse must sign a statement agreeing to that. If you die before retirement, your spouse may not receive any of your retirement benefit.

Keep in mind that employers most often pay for the QPSA. If this is the case, you will probably not be able to exclude yourself.

May single people enroll for the QPSA?

The QPSA is designed to protect a spouse. There is no benefit for single people. Be careful, though: enrollment may be automatic. You may not even be aware of it, but you could be paying for something you can't use!

―――――――――→ ACTION ITEM ←―――――――――

If you are single, contact your benefits representative and determine whether you are paying for something you don't need, by being enrolled in the QPSA.

―――――――――――――――――――――――――――

―――――――――― **POINTS TO REMEMBER** ――――――――――

▸ Many, but not all, retirement plans protect the spouses of workers under the qualified preretirement survivor annuity (QPSA). The QPSA pays a benefit to the spouse of a worker who dies while still actively employed.

▸ Some people decline the spousal coverage because, without it, retired employees receive a higher living benefit. If you elect out of participating in the QPSA, however, your spouse will receive nothing if you die while still employed.

▶ QPSAs are an expensive benefit. Employers must decide whether they want to absorb this cost or pass it on to the employees.

▶ If you are using the payroll deduction method to purchase the QPSA, at retirement you may receive a portion of your retirement benefit tax-free.

▶ Generally, under the QPSA, if you die, your spouse will receive 50 percent of your vested benefit, starting in the year you would have reached retirement age.

▶ Purchasing life insurance may be a less expensive way to provide the same protection as the QPSA for your spouse.

▶ Single people cannot benefit from a QPSA.

18

Getting Started with Retirement Income

*L*earning about retirement plans and the rules regarding distributions is admirable. For some people, it's even fun! But what's the use of knowing all this information, unless you do something with it?

The book's remaining chapters encourage you to use the information you have been pulling together. As you go through these chapters, your retirement finances will become clear, and you will understand how simple decisions can greatly impact these finances.

These are active chapters. Before you continue reading, get a pad of paper and a pencil, and maybe a calculator. Sit at a table or desk, so that you'll have room for the book, your worksheets, and reference materials such as your benefits statement. Have a good overhead light. Give yourself at least a half-hour of uninterrupted time, so that you'll be able to dig in!

If you find yourself saying, "Gee, I never did very well with arithmetic," don't worry: these "exercises" weren't created by professors. Nearly all are ideas brought to us by real people from all walks of life. What they had in common was a desire to understand and make their own decisions. A few points before we begin:

▶ Get your information out of your head and down on paper!

▶ Label your lists and calculations. Don't worry about using official terms or titles; these chapters are for your benefit, so call things what you want. But don't omit labels. It might be hard to remember what you were doing, a couple of weeks or months from now. Your worksheets will be *useless* to people you consult, if they aren't properly labeled.

▶ You'll need to redo your worksheets as information changes. To avoid confusing your new and your previous worksheets, develop the habit of dating *every* worksheet *each time* you work on it.

OVERVIEW OF THE PLANNING PROCESS

We'll start in this chapter by determining the income you can expect at retirement. We'll look at specific income items, such as your retirement plan, social security, income from investments, and so on. We'll put these together onto one page and call it "Retirement Income Worksheet."

In Chapter 19, we'll explore ways to enhance your retirement income for you and your survivors. These often overlooked methods may put some extra money in your pocket! In Chapter 20, we'll work on a "Retirement Expenses Worksheet." In Chapter 21, we'll combine retirement income and expenses, and end up with a modest financial plan. Chapter 21 will give you the insight to look at your retirement over a long period of time, under varying conditions and circumstances. We'll show you how to play "what if" games.

Your goal in these chapters is to be able to measure the long-term impact of your decisions on your retirement life-style.

LET'S GET STARTED!

Identifying sources of retirement income should be easy, if you've read the earlier chapters that apply to you. Now it's time to convert general information to actual numbers and dates, and to develop a complete Retirement Income Worksheet.

If you are like most people, your retirement income will come from several sources. Having read this book, you've probably identified most sources, but you may have others we haven't talked about.

HOW MUCH INCOME TO EXPECT

This book is largely devoted to helping you anticipate your retirement income. All sources of income need to be looked at and measured differently.

⎯⎯⎯⎯⎯⎯⎯→ ACTION ITEM ←⎯⎯⎯⎯⎯⎯⎯

Here's a pretty complete list of possible sources of income. Put a check mark (✓) next to each source of income you expect to have.

Sources of retirement income:

_____ **Wages**

_____ **Income from self-employment**

_____ **Monthly pension**

_____ **Investment income from lump-sum retirement plan payout**

_____ **Social security**

_____ **Interest from savings**

_____ **Dividends**

_____ **Distributions from IRAs or other retirement savings plans you control**

_____ **Income from rental real estate**

_____ **Income from trusts (set up by parents, for example)**

_____ **Other** _____

When looking at your income, don't forget that couples may have separate income from several sources. *Each* of you may need to do a worksheet. For example, it might be helpful, when checking off the list, to make two columns of check marks, one for each person.

Having identified your sources of income, let's look at each.

STARTING WITH WAGES AND SELF-EMPLOYMENT INCOME

We are starting with job income. Does this mean you should continue to work? There's no "right answer" to this question. However, we have found that people who move quickly into a second career, whether or not it pays the same as their first one, are often healthier and happier in retirement. Although it may not be financially necessary, it may be desirable for you to continue to work during your retirement.

Remember that continuing to work *for the same employer* may endanger your retired status, particularly the special treatment of lump-sum distributions.

JEOPARDIZING SOCIAL SECURITY

Continuing to work could jeopardize your social security: under current rules, you can only earn a limited amount from working, before social security begins to be taken away. (Social security is a retirement benefit, and working people aren't considered retired.)

In 1992, if you are under age 65, you can earn up to $7,440 income from working and keep all of your social security benefits. From age 65 to age 70, the amount increases to $10,200. After age 70, you can earn all the income you want from working, without losing any of your social security benefits. (These dollar limits go up each year.)

Remember, for social security purposes, earned income is money you make by your *labor*. Earned income does not include income from pensions, interest, dividends, capital gains, or rental property.

WEALTH   *The Last Haul.* Tom, a retired truck driver, dropped
BUILDING   in to have lunch with his son. While he was waiting,
PROFILE   he chatted with the receptionist.

"What's it like, not having to work any more?" she asked eagerly. "Must be wonderful . . . ."

"Well, I'll let you know next month," replied Tom. "I still have another run to make before I'm through for this year."

"What do you mean," she asked. "I thought you retired in January. You're getting social security, aren't you?"

"Yep," Tom admitted. "But I can still work and make some money and keep all my social security, too. That's what I mean about my last run. When I finish this one, I'll have made just up to this year's limit. Then I'll *really* retire!"

➔ ACTION ITEM ◆

Begin your research on working after retirement. Remember, working may not meet financial needs so much as it fulfills personal lifetime goals. You may want to talk with a career counselor, or take a class in building a résumé, as part of your research. Keep in mind that your social security income may be affected by your income from working.

PLANNING AROUND A MONTHLY PENSION

Nearly all of Chapter 12 deals with pension payout options. Refer to it for review as necessary.

You already know that, if you leave a pension benefit to a spouse or other survivor, your own benefit will be less. Table 18–1 will help you decide which option is best.

We start with a simple example. Jim is retiring. He wants to be sure that, if he dies, his wife June will be protected. June has no pension of her own.

First, let's look at the three scenarios that Jim and June might expect. Scenario A is their situation at retirement, when both are alive; scenario B assumes Jim has died; scenario C assumes June dies before Jim.

Next, we fill in the pension payout choices from Jim's retirement plan. We can see the exact income either or both will have, depending on the payout choices they make and the way their life spans turn out.

Jim and June choose the joint and survivor (J & S) 100 percent (boldface in Table 18–1). They feel that neither the single life nor the J & S 50 percent would leave enough for June to live on, if Jim dies first. They begin their planning using the J & S 100 percent as their first choice; the J & S 66²/₃ percent is a potential second choice. They will make their final decision after looking at their other sources of income.

Again, if you and your spouse *both* have pensions, you will have to expand your worksheet. If you are single, your worksheet will be greatly simplified.

Make a chart for each pension in your family. By stacking them, you can combine income from each pension for each scenario. You may have to play with different combinations, to get the best result for your circumstances.

Table 18–1
Pension Choices

Scenario→	A: Jim and June Together	B: June Alone	C: Jim Alone
Payout Choices:			
Single life	$655/mo.	$ 0	$655
J & S 50%	615	307	615
J & S 66 2/3%	586	390	586
J & S 100%	**560**	560	560

Be sure to fill in your own scenarios. Our example shows a husband and wife in the traditional situation, but your family circumstances may be very different. For example, you may have a dependent other than a spouse; you may be responsible for a divorced spouse; you may be single now, but planning to get married. Whatever the case, adjust your chart to fit *your* situation. Table 18–2 is a useful form to get you started.

Table 18–2
Pension Choices Chart

Pension #1 from	Scenarios at Retirement		
(Employer)	A	B	C
Payout options			
1. _____	_____	_____	_____
2. _____	_____	_____	_____
3. _____	_____	_____	_____
4. _____	_____	_____	_____
5. _____	_____	_____	_____

Pension #2 from

(Employer)			
Payout options			
1. _____	_____	_____	_____
2. _____	_____	_____	_____
3. _____	_____	_____	_____
4. _____	_____	_____	_____
Total pension income*	_____	_____	_____

* Put an asterisk beside the option from each pension that seems best to you. Combine your choices on this line.

————————————→ **ACTION ITEM** ←————————————

Create your own pension choices chart, imitating Figure 18–2. List the scenarios along the top. Down the left side, list the pension payout options available to you through your retirement plan. You may have some of those listed above, but you may have others, too, including a period-certain option (such as a 10-year period-certain). Then fill in the amounts.

Make a first choice from each pension and combine the choices on the Total Pension Income line.

APPLYING FOR SOCIAL SECURITY

The idea of "a bird in the hand is worth two in the bush" applies very well to social security. A simple calculation shows that, if you wait until age 65 to draw your social security, it takes about 12 years before the higher (age 65) payment makes up for the 3 years when you didn't receive anything (ages 62 to 65).

Your spouse should probably apply for social security at age 62, too, but there is an interesting twist to the spousal benefit. To explain it, let's review how the social security payment works.

Social security is a retirement benefit payable to people who have worked under the system for at least 10 years. A retiree can receive the highest benefit starting at age 65, with a reduced benefit available as early as age 62.

Unlike a pension, social security provides for a spousal benefit to be paid *at the same time* the worker's benefit is paid. It is paid to the spouse of a worker, based on the worker's record. Spouses who have themselves worked thus have a choice to make: should they take the "worker's benefit" (their own) or the "spousal benefit," based on their spouse's record? The answer depends on which benefit is larger. The spousal benefit is about 50 percent of the worker's benefit, with both adjusted for inflation each year.

The twist works this way. Let's say you have worked for 30 full years under the social security system. Your spouse has worked only on and off, but still meets the 10-year minimum. As you reach retirement, your spouse retires first and begins to draw the worker's benefit at age 62. Let's say it amounts to $185.

Now it's your turn to retire. You are 65 years old. You apply for your benefit, which turns out to be $800 per month. Your spouse now may switch from the worker's benefit to a spousal benefit. Remember, your spouse is eligible for either. In this case, your spouse's benefit goes from $185 to $400! Not a bad raise!

These rules apply equally for men and women.

As you approach retirement, if your circumstances are, in any way, out of the ordinary (just about everyone's are), request a review with the social security office nearest you. If you have been married, divorced, or widowed, or have dependent children or disabled dependents, check with social security to receive your highest benefit. Remember, social security has different categories of benefits, and you may fit more than one!

If your circumstances change, let social security know immediately. You may have changed categories and become entitled to a higher benefit.

Social security rules change regularly, as do the amounts being paid to retirees. The best way for you to keep in touch with your own benefit is to call the new social security hotline. Dial 1-800-772-1213 to request Form SSA-7004. Fill it out and send it in. Within a couple of weeks, your work history and your estimated retirement benefit will be sent to you.

─────────────→ **ACTION ITEM** ←─────────────

Call now to request Form SSA-7004 for your estimated social security retirement benefit. The hotline number is 1-800-772-1213. When you've received your information, fill in these blanks: My/our estimated Social Security Benefit will be $_____ starting in (year) _____.

USING INTEREST AND DIVIDEND INCOME AT RETIREMENT

Fortunately, many people reinvest interest, dividends, and capital gains while they are working, allowing the money to accumulate and grow. We discussed earlier in the book the power of compounding interest. In retirement, compounding will probably become an important source of income. It's wise to know what to expect.

Use the worksheet in Table 18–3 to get a better idea of the interest, dividends, and capital gains you're earning. In the left column, list bank accounts, stocks, and mutual funds. What interest rate are your savings accounts earning? What are the stocks and mutual funds paying over the course of a year? Use the last column to divide by 12, converting your income to a monthly figure.

Bonds could be put under the category "Interest-Bearing Accounts and Values," or you may wish to add a third section titled "Bonds and Bond Mutual Funds."

When you complete your worksheet, you will have identified a potential source of extra retirement income. Most people reinvest as long as they can, and then convert the interest and dividends to spendable income, often account-by-account.

The goal is to identify all potential sources of retirement income. It doesn't matter how they are arranged!

Table 18–3
Worksheet for Interest and Dividends Income

Interest-Bearing Accounts and Values	Interest Income Currently Earning ____%	Annual Income	Monthly Income
1. _____	_____	_____	_____
2. _____	_____	_____	_____
3. _____	_____	_____	_____
4. _____	_____	_____	_____
5. _____	_____	_____	_____

Dividends and Capital Gains from Stock or Mutual Funds	Annual Income	Monthly Income
1. _____	_____	_____
2. _____	_____	_____
3. _____	_____	_____
4. _____	_____	_____
5. _____	_____	_____

RECEIVING MONTHLY INTEREST
AND DIVIDEND INCOME

The worksheet in Table 18–3 converts the interest and dividends to a monthly figure, because all other planning has been done on a monthly basis. In reality, interest, dividends, and capital gains may be paid out monthly, quarterly, twice a year, once a year, or even only after several years, as in the case of some certificates of deposits.

By the same token, many household bills are paid quarterly, semi-annually, or annually—automobile insurance, property tax, and so on. The best retirement budget will be a month-by-month budget, showing not only the month-by-month regular expenses, but also the irregular ones.

─────────────→ **ACTION ITEM** ←─────────────
Make a list of your investments that earn interest, dividends, or capital gains. Convert this income to a monthly figure, for initial planning.

WITHDRAWALS FROM
RETIREMENT PLANS

Withdrawals from IRAs and other retirement plans *must* begin by age 70$\frac{1}{2}$. Review Chapter 14 for rules regarding minimum withdrawal.

Getting the money out may be as simple as requesting a withdrawal by phone. If you have several IRAs or different retirement plans, however, and have postponed your withdrawals until the last minute, completing the withdrawals on time can be very complicated.

Remember, the rule is that you must withdraw the required amount from *the total value* of your IRA accounts (including SEPs and CODAs), each year after you reach age 70$\frac{1}{2}$. Withdrawals from TSAs, 401(k)s, ESOPs, and Keoghs must be figured separately.

Your first step is to add the values of all your IRAs as of year-end. Apply the proper life expectancy figure, to get the exact withdrawal amount. Next, pick the best IRA or IRAs to take the money from. (Remember, you must withdraw a minimum amount from non-IRA-type retirement plans, too.)

Be sure to request the withdrawal in plenty of time. Nearly all trustees have forms that you must fill out before they'll release the money.

WEALTH   ***Timing Is Everything!*** Evelyn reached 70¹/₂ in
BUILDING   March of this year. She knows she'll have to make her
PROFILE   first IRA withdrawal by April 1 of next year, so she
assembles her IRA information.

Evelyn is single. When she checks the minimum withdrawal chart, she finds that her required withdrawal is 6.3 percent. She multiplies the total value of the IRAs, $19,000, by 6.3 percent and comes up with a minimum requirement of $1,197.

IRA Account Values

Where the IRA Is	*Account #*	*Value as of 12/31/____*	*Withdrawal Restrictions*
Credit union	#1234	$13,500	Quarterly withdr.
Local bank	#11111	4,300	No restrictions
Local S & L	#222	1,200	Matures 3/26
TOTAL		$19,000	

Which account should she take the money from? It makes sense to simplify her life, so she decides to clear out the S & L IRA. However, that account has a penalty for withdrawal before maturity. If she waits until the certificate matures, she'll have just 5 days to make the withdrawal, to avoid a penalty from either the bank or the IRS!

PLANNING AROUND CERTIFICATES OF DEPOSIT (CDs)

If your retirement plan money is in a timed deposit, wait until the account matures, then request that the appropriate amount be sent to you. Allow the rest to stay in the retirement plan and earn interest. If you have to withdraw money in any given year, be sure the account matures sometime within that year. In that way, you won't be faced with interest penalties for breaking the timed deposit!

→ **ACTION ITEM** ←

List your IRA and other retirement plan accounts. Be sure to note withdrawal restrictions for each account. If you expect to make withdrawals soon, decide which accounts to make them from. You may want to set up a withdrawal calendar, building in plenty of time for paperwork.

PUTTING IT ALL TOGETHER

Put all your income on one page and label the page Monthly Retirement Income. Start with your first year of retirement. The worksheet in Figure 18–1 shows how to lay it out.

→ **ACTION ITEM** ←

Complete an estimated Monthly Retirement Income worksheet for the first year of your retirement.

Monthly Retirement Income   Year _____

Source	Jan.	Feb.	Mar.	Apr.	May		Nov.	Dec.	Totals
Salary/wages									
Retirement 1									
Retirement 2									
Social security									
Interest									
Dividends									
Rents									
IRA withdrawal									
Other									
TOTALS									

Note: Assign a month to the omitted columns.

Figure 18–1

Worksheet for estimating your retirement income.

?

I'd like to figure my social security myself. Any suggestions?

There is no simple formula for determining your social security benefit. We recommend you simply use the estimates available through Form SSA-7004. However, you may wish to buy one of the more detailed books about social security, available at bookstores. One of them will surely have a worksheet that meets your needs. Be sure you get the very latest edition.

One of my IRAs is invested with an insurance company. Are the payout procedures any different from those of a bank or a mutual fund?

You may receive a reminder letter from your trustee, offering you distribution choices. For example, you may be asked to choose a payout based on your life expectancy, or on your and your spouse's combined life expectancy. Or, the trustee may offer you an installment-type payment spread over, say, 10 years.

Usually, the trustee's letter only includes the institution's choices, and the one you want may not be listed. If this is the case, you may have to write a letter giving appropriate instructions.

Remember, it's your money, and you're the only one who knows your situation. Don't let official-sounding documents sway you into making a poor, or possibly wrong, choice. It's your tax liability, too!

I have several IRAs. How can I simplify my retirement plan withdrawals?

As you approach the time to make withdrawals from your retirement plans, it may be convenient to use the IRA rollover or a trustee-to-trustee transfer, to combine them under one trustee. (Remember, the IRA rollover rule allows you to combine different retirement plans under one IRA.)

It may be practical to roll over or transfer your accounts to a mutual fund or other investment that allows a systematic withdrawal. Decide on the amount you wish to withdraw each year; then give instructions for the mutual fund to send you a check each month for $1/12$ of that amount. For example, if you wanted $3,000 over the course of a year, the monthly check would be $250.

Aren't mutual funds risky?

A mutual fund is a large pool of money invested according to rules. These rules are clearly laid out in the mutual fund prospectus. (Despite its imposing-sounding name, the prospectus is merely a pamphlet describing the fund, its charges, and how to deposit and withdraw money. The prospectus usually includes an application.)

Each mutual fund has a different set of rules. For example, one mutual fund may be invested only in the stock of "emerging companies." That type of fund may be quite risky. Other mutual funds are invested only in CDs, or other banking instruments, including U.S. Government Treasury Bills. These mutual funds, called money market funds, are among the safest investments.

Mutual funds have the ability to create for you a monthly income from your retirement plan. Such convenient withdrawal programs are worth the extra research that often goes into learning about them.

--------------------→ **ACTION ITEM** ←--------------------

Review your retirement plan investments. Consider combining them into one or two IRA accounts, using the IRA rollover or trustee-to-trustee transfer. If a regular monthly distribution fits your income goals, find out about using a mutual fund's systematic distribution program.

What about other sources of income?

We've touched on the most common sources of retirement income. Some retirees also have income from rental real estate, trusts, inheritances, or sale of assets. Often, this income and the time of receipt must be estimated. Our only advice here is to be conservative in your estimate or even exclude the income for planning purposes, until you actually receive it. Furthermore, don't overlook the possibility that taxes may be owed on this money and you must plan for their payment.

One tax-free source of income that is gaining in popularity is known as a reverse mortgage or reverse amortization loan. This type of financing allows older homeowners to "unlock" the equity that has built up in their homes, changing it to a fixed monthly income for as long as they stay in the house. These loans are very new, and variations are occurring regularly. For the latest information, consult with a mortgage broker or banker.

POINTS TO REMEMBER

▶ Give yourself the time and tools to do in-depth analysis of your retirement income.

▶ The first step is to list all sources of retirement income for each family member.

▶ Working while drawing social security may reduce your social security payment up to age 70.

▶ Consider all your pension payout options. Be sure to look at the worst case as well as the best case.

▶ For most people, it makes sense to apply for social security as soon as they reach age 62, the minimum age when social security payments can begin.

▶ Social security makes payments to retired workers, spouses of retired workers, and widows or widowers. It is important to keep the Social Security Administration up to date with changes in your circumstances, to be sure you are getting all you are entitled to.

▶ There is no easy way to estimate social security benefits. Contact the Social Security Administration on a regular basis, to find out their latest figures for you.

▶ Identify interest and dividends that you are earning and reinvesting. In retirement, you may wish to use this income to meet current expenses.

▶ Time your required withdrawals from your IRA or other retirement plans, to avoid IRS penalties for late distribution *and* potential banking or insurance penalties for "breaking" timed deposits.

▶ For simplicity's sake, consider combining all your retirement accounts into one or two IRAs, using the IRA rollover or trustee-to-trustee transfer.

19

Enhancing Your Retirement Income Using Life Insurance

*A*fter looking at your retirement income, you may find that your pension does not offer exactly what you want, in the way of payout choices or survivor benefits. If this is the case, you may be able to increase your options by using the often overlooked method of enhancing retirement income with life insurance.

Years ago, the concept of retirement income enchancement (sometimes called pension maximization) using life insurance usually did not work. Life insurance was not competitive with retirement plan payout options. Today's insurance products, however, may give you a way to increase your planning flexibility and improve your retirement paycheck.

There is no simple way to know whether pension enhancement will work for you or whether it won't. The only way to know is to do an analysis. This chapter covers the subject step-by-step.

HOW PENSION
ENHANCEMENT WORKS

Pension enhancement works this way. At retirement, elect a higher retirement payout—say, a J & S 50 percent rather than a J & S 100 percent. Purchase a life insurance policy with a portion of this income. At your death, your survivor receives the insurance proceeds and invests them to produce income *in addition to* the survivor's retirement benefit. The two sources of income may be higher than a survivor's benefit alone would have been. While you are alive, the higher retirement plan payout may increase your monthly income, even after subtracting the cost of the insurance premiums!

Furthermore, if you live a long life, certain life insurance policies build up a cash value. This cash value may later be withdrawn for more retirement income.

The arguments for this approach depend on the newer, higher-interest-rate life insurance policies (Universal Life, Interest-Sensitive Whole Life, and so on). The risk you run is in giving up a sure thing (your pension) for something with many variables:

▶ How long will the insurance proceeds last?

▶ What interest rate will they be able to earn?

▶ Will there be any chance of losing the money?

These questions, and others, make deciding about pension enhancement somewhat difficult. Not everyone will use the method, but everyone should at least consider it. Rejecting the idea is valid, if it is not appropriate for you. What is not acceptable is recognizing, years from now, that it could have worked and you could have been many dollars ahead.

JOINT AND SURVIVOR
VERSUS INSURANCE

If you are protecting a survivor, your retirement income is already being reduced. You may look at the reduction to protect your survivor as a form of insurance premium. The reduction "cost" could have been used to purchase different insurance; rather than J & S protection, it could have purchased a life insurance policy. To illustrate, we have expanded Table 12–1 and included a column headed Cost of Protecting Survivor. Table 19–1 shows the expanded analysis.

With the information from the Action Item on page 217, you can determine how much life insurance is needed to replace a portion of your retirement benefit.

First, how much income will you be receiving from your retirement plan? Let's say the joint and survivor 50 percent option will

Table 19–1
Cost of Protecting a Survivor: Sample Single Life and Joint Retirement Payouts

	Joint and Survivor[1]	Survivor Only[2]	Cost of Protecting Survivor
Single life	$500	$ 0	$ 0
J & S 50%	$400	$200	$100[3]
J & S 100%	$350	$350	$150[4]

[1] Employee's and survivor's retirement benefit.
[2] Survivor's benefit for life (except 10-year certain) if employee dies after retirement.
[3] Difference between single life and J & S 50%.
[4] Difference between single life and J & S 100%.

———————————→ **ACTION ITEM** ←———————————
Use the blank form below to create a chart similar to the one shown in Table 19–1. Determine from your payout options your cost of protecting a survivor.

	Joint and Survivor[1]	Survivor Only[2]	Cost of Protecting Survivor
Single life	$_____	$ 0	$_____
J & S 50%	$_____	$_____	$_____[3]
J & S 100%	$_____	$_____	$_____[4]

[1] Employee's and survivor's retirement benefit.
[2] Survivor's benefit for life (except 10-year certain) if employee dies after retirement.
[3] Difference between single life and J & S 50%.
[4] Difference between single life and J & S 100%.

produce $400 to you while you are alive and, after your death, $200 (50 percent) for the remaining life of your survivor. Further, let's say that the joint and survivor 100 percent option will produce $350 to you while you are alive *or* to your survivor after your death.

Thus, a $50 monthly income reduction ($350 instead of $400) ensures that your survivor will receive an additional $150 per month ($350 rather than $200).

Next, answer this question: for $50 per month, could you purchase enough life insurance to safely produce $150 per month for the rest of your survivor's life?

To answer the question, you would need to know two things:

▸ The life expectancy of your survivor;

▸ The rate of return your survivor could safely receive from the insurance proceeds, without the possibility of loss of capital.

Because you cannot know these things, any answer you give to the question will be only a guess. Yet, you are facing enormous risks related to the pension enhancement method. What if your survivor lives longer than anticipated? What if your survivor can't achieve the rate of return originally estimated? You need to add a safety margin, to be sure your answers don't put your survivor at risk.

Table 12–2 has presented experts' estimates of average life expectancies at various ages. Table 19–2 illustrates how long money will last, when it is earning a constant interest rate and is being withdrawn at a specific dollar rate each month.

For our illustration, assume your survivor is going to live 30 years, and you can earn 6 percent interest with no risk. Table 19–2 shows that you would need to purchase $25,000 of life insurance to protect your survivor.

Once you know the amount of life insurance you need, it becomes a matter of researching the various *types* of insurance available and the companies providing them. This, of course, is no small task!

WHEN TO CONSIDER INSURANCE

If the idea works for retirement-age people, you can usually save money by buying life insurance at a younger age in anticipation of future retirement. Generally, the younger you are, the less your life insurance will cost, although many factors other than age enter into determining life insurance premiums.

Another reason for considering this alternative is to protect your heirs. Retirement planning often overlooks the death of both you and your survivor. In this event, your heirs generally receive nothing from your pension. If you have purchased insurance, however, and both you and your spouse die, your heirs will very likely receive a larger inheritance.

WEALTH
BUILDING
PROFILE

Increasing Your Retirement Benefit. Clay is 62 years old and thinking of retiring. He and his wife, Shelly, have already talked to the company benefits representative and understand the various retirement payout options. They also want to see how life insurance could fit into their plans.

Their insurance agent, Eileen, pays them a visit.

Eileen quickly points out that if Clay and Shelly elect the J & S 50 percent option, at Clay's death Shelly will receive 50 percent of what they had jointly been receiving. The joint benefit amounts to $600 per month. Shelly's monthly benefit would be $300 at the time of Clay's death.

If they elect the J & S 100 percent option, their joint benefit will be $525 per month ($75 less than the 50 percent option). At Clay's death, however, Shelly will continue to receive $525.

Eileen summarizes, "You are paying $75 per month to the retirement plan to guarantee that Shelly will receive an extra $225 per month if Clay dies." She continues, "If Clay lives a long life, you will continue to pay that $75 out and not receive anything back as a benefit. I believe my company can offer you the same protection at a lower cost and, if you live long, it may return money to you in the form of cash values."

They continue their study. If they choose the 50 percent J & S option, with the highest monthly benefit ($600), they can purchase an insurance policy from Eileen for $50 per month which will meet their needs. Their situation will look like this:

▶ Clay and Shelly will have $25 per month more in their pocket (over the J & S 100 percent option), even after paying the insurance premium.

▶ If Clay should die, Shelly will receive $35,000 in insurance proceeds which, if invested at 6 percent, will generate $225 of income per month for Shelly for 25 years.

▶ If Clay lives a long life, they will be accumulating cash value in their insurance policy, which can be drawn on in later years.

▶ If Shelly dies prematurely, Clay can stop making payments to the insurance company because the protection need is no longer there. Thus, he will have more income to spend.

They agree to purchase the life insurance policy and pick the J & S 50 percent option at their retirement interview.

━━━━━━━━━━━━━➤ **ACTION ITEM** ◀━━━━━━━━
Evaluate your situation to see whether combining life insurance with a higher pension payout makes sense. Use the profile of Clay and Shelly as a guide. Remember, the younger you are when you purchase it, the less your insurance will cost.

IF YOUR SURVIVOR DIES
BEFORE YOU DO

If your survivor dies while you are still working, choose the single life option when you are ready to retire. This gives you the highest benefit possible—but it leaves nothing for survivors. You may change the beneficiary on your enhancement insurance, to transfer the benefit, or you may decide to stop paying for the insurance.

If you have already retired, the option you chose at retirement (i.e., J & S 50 percent or J & S 100 percent option) will most likely be the option you will live with for the rest of your life. In a few cases, the plan reduces the benefit paid to the retired employee at the survivor's death to survivor status. As for the insurance, you will have the opportunity to reconsider its value to you in your new circumstances. If it was only meant to protect the beneficiary who died, you may wish to cancel the policy.

THE RESTORE OPTION

A few plans offer an additional option commonly known as the "restore" option. This allows the surviving employee to step back into the single life benefit if the survivor dies first.

Remember, not all plans offer this option. If yours does offer this option, it may not be apparent from reading the benefits statement. To find out whether this option is available, you may have to read your benefits booklets or talk to a benefits representative.

As mentioned before, if the survivor dies before the retired employee, the restore option allows the employee to go back to or restore the single life benefit. The retired employee's income increases because only one life is now covered.

→ ACTION ITEM ←

It is important to understand the survivor options available to you (the retired employee), should your survivor die before you. To help you understand them, ask your benefits representative these questions:

▶ **What are the survivor benefits if the retired employee is the survivor?**

▶ **Is a restore option available?**

At the time you retire, your benefits representative should ask whether you want to pay for the restore option by reducing your J & S benefit for the rest of your life. This *ensures* that, if your survivor dies before you, you will be able to go back to a single life benefit.

→ ACTION ITEM ←

If your pension has a restore option, before you sign up for it, find out how much your retirement benefit will be reduced.

DESIGN YOUR OWN
RESTORE OPTION

You can design your own restore option by purchasing life insurance on your survivor. If that person dies before you do, you'll receive the insurance proceeds. These proceeds can be invested and then paid out to you over several years. Thus, the income you receive from the life insurance proceeds could bring your total retirement income up to the single life benefit.

As you compare costs, keep in mind that the restore option *is* a type of life insurance policy. You pay the premiums by a reduction in your retirement plan's benefits. At the death of your survivor, the proceeds go to the pension plan rather than to you. There, they produce enough income to boost your retirement to the single life benefit.

Additionally, by using insurance, you can insure for any income you desire, either more or less than the single life benefit.

WEALTH   *Understanding Your Situation.* Maggie's retire-
BUILDING   ment was coming up, and she was facing the decision
PROFILE   of which payout option to choose. Would she outlive
                   her husband or would her husband outlive her? His
family did have a history of heart disease, but, according to his last physical, he was in good shape. Because everyone in her family lived into their 90s, she knew she would need the highest possible retirement payout. If she died prematurely, however, she wanted her husband to receive a portion of her retirement benefit. Thus, a joint and survivor option was necessary while her husband was alive.

After discussing this with the company benefits people, Maggie felt she should consider the restore option. It allowed her to know that, if she died early, her husband would be protected. Or, if her husband were to die, she could step back into the single life benefit. The only thing left was to determine whether the cost was reasonable for her needs.

She continued to analyze her retirement. She found that her single life benefit amounted to $525 per month; the joint and survivor 100 percent option reduced her monthly income to $368, but guaranteed her spouse $368 if she died. By electing the restore option, she would pay $43 per month out of her joint and survivor option, but she knew she would receive $525 per month if her husband died.

She wondered if, for $43 per month, the restore option was worth the difference in income ($368 to $525, or a difference of $157). For $43 per month, she might be able to buy an insurance policy on her husband that, if he died, could give her enough money to generate $157 per month. After all, he should easily qualify for insurance; if he did die and she could earn 6 percent on the money, she would only need about $25,000 of insurance. This would last her for at least 25 years.

Checking with her insurance company, she found she could purchase a $25,000 Universal Life policy for $35 per month. The policy would build up cash values if her husband lived. At $35 per month, it was a savings over the restore option and had the added benefit of cash value buildup!

The decision became easy once she did her investigation.

?

Are there other advantages to using insurance for protection of income, rather than a restore option?

The primary purpose of life insurance is to produce additional income if your survivor dies before you. Additionally, in the event you die after your survivor, the insurance proceeds will be in your estate for the benefit of your heirs or charity. The single life option does not allow any income to go to heirs or charity.

Are there any advantages to using the restore option over insurance?

The restore option is a guaranteed option that usually does not require any medical examination. If your survivor could not pass a life insurance medical exam, the restore option is a good choice.

How much will life insurance cost? (See Table 19–2.)

The cost depends primarily on age and health. Generally, the younger the insured, the less it will cost. The cost also varies by type (term or cash value).

What are the risks of pension enhancement?

First, you must be careful that your assumptions are correct and that the insurance you purchase will yield the results it is supposed to. An insurance policy with high internal fees may not hold its value, if interest rates change dramatically over the years you have it. Be sure you understand how to evaluate your policy.

Table 19-2
Insurance Needs with Constant Interest and Withdrawal Amounts

	Amount of Insurance								
	$25,000			$50,000			$75,000		
Rate of Return	Monthly Income Need								
	$150	$250	$500	$150	$250	$500	$150	$250	$500
	Length of time income will last, in years*								
5%	24	11	5	**	36	11	**	**	20
6	30	12	5	**	**	12	**	**	23
7	51	13	5	**	**	13	**	**	30
8	**	14	5	**	**	14	**	**	**
9	**	15	5	**	**	15	**	**	**
10	**	18	5	**	**	18	**	**	**

	Amount of Insurance								
	$100,000			$150,000			$200,000		
Rate of Return	Monthly Income Need								
	$500	$1,000	$1,500	$500	$1,000	$1,500	$500	$1,000	$1,500
	Length of time income will last in years*								
5%	36	11	7	**	20	11	**	36	16
6	**	12	7	**	23	12	**	**	18
7	**	13	7	**	30	13	**	**	22
8	**	14	7	**	**	14	**	**	28
9	**	15	8	**	**	15	**	**	**
10	**	18	8	**	**	18	**	**	**

* Rounded to the nearest year.
** Income will last forever.

Second, the person inheriting the policy could outlive his or her planned life expectancy, or may not be able to invest the money to earn as much interest as you had planned. Be sure you use very conservative figures when you do your planning, to allow for these possibilities.

How often does pension enhancement really make sense?

Each company retirement plan operates with different assumptions; some plans lend themselves to enhancement and some don't. As you study your plan, you will know clearly whether pension enhancement works for you. There is no way to know for sure without doing the analysis.

If I am single, does it make sense for me to protect my pension benefit with insurance?

If you have chosen the single life benefit, and you die, no one will receive a benefit beyond your death. To leave your pension benefit to someone, you will have to choose a joint and survivor option or use a portion of your retirement benefit to purchase a life insurance policy. Purchasing a life insurance policy may be a better choice if you choose the type of policy that builds a cash value. That way, should you live a long life, the cash value can add to your own retirement income in later years.

POINTS TO REMEMBER

▶ If your retirement income, or your spouse's income, isn't sufficient, you may wish to consider pension enhancement. Choose a higher pension payout, then purchase life insurance on your life which can be used after your death to supplement your spouse's lower retirement plan benefit. Good health and a good policy may combine to give your spouse more than he or she would have had by simply receiving the survivor benefit.

▶ Pension enhancement may be a way for single people to leave a benefit to a chosen beneficiary when the joint and survivor option is unavailable.

▶ Pension enhancement gives retirees more retirement income if their designated survivor dies before they do.

▶ Using life insurance may leave money for heirs or charity; a joint and survivor payout stops with the death of the second person.

20

Retirement
Expenses

*B*egin to gather information that will be important when you plan your retirement expenses. This chapter discusses some of the obvious and not-so-obvious changes you can expect. The goal of the chapter is to arrive at a preliminary Monthly Retirement Expenses worksheet.

Some people may want to fit in an intermediate step, before they tackle the actual worksheet. If you haven't been keeping track of your expenses, use Figure 20–1, a Monthly Expense Record, to get started. Make several copies, label them by month, and begin to record your spending.

Over the years we've heard good suggestions for being sure that important things weren't missed. Here are the best ones:

▶ Write checks for everything, including a $2 expense. You'll have a good record, and you may even decide to do without some expenses, just because of the nuisance!

▶ Charge larger items on a credit card. Again, you'll have an easy, accurate record of your expenses. Be sure to pay off the bill each month, to avoid finance charges.

▶ Carry a small book for recording your cash purchases. Collect and save receipts. Be diligent! If you wait until the end of the day to try to remember everything, you'll probably miss something!

Monthly Expense Record

Month _____ Year _____

Date	Savings	Mortgage/Rent	Food	Clothing	Medical		Business Related	Other: Taxes
Totals								

Note: Suggested additional column headings: Household Operation, Utilities, Transportation, Child Care, Debts, Insurance, Education, Personal Care, Recreation, Gifts.

——————— **Figure 20–1** ———————

Worksheet for calculating expenses per month.

Monthly Retirement Expenses   Year _____

Item	Jan.	Feb.	Mar.	Apr.	May		Nov.	Dec.	Totals
Mortgage/rent									
Maintenance									
Property tax									
Utilities									
Food									
Eating out									
Clothing									
Entertainment									
Transportation									
Medical + ins.									
Education									
Travel/leisure									
Gifts									
Personal care									
Business exp.									
Save/contrib.									
Income taxes									
Soc. Sec. tax									
Other									
TOTALS									

Note: Assign a month to the omitted columns.

--------------------------- **Figure 20-2** ---------------------------
Worksheet for estimating your retirement expenses.

▶ Approach record keeping as a fun exercise. Set a time limit (say, 3 months), but give yourself plenty of time to get this portion of your planning accomplished. Allow enough time that you won't feel overwhelmed.

▶ Ask around. Find out how other people are keeping records. You'll be surprised at how many people do this kind of record keeping month-in and month-out! Many set up record keeping as their first project on a home computer.

Again, the goal of the exercise is to understand your spending patterns. When they become clear, retirement planning will be a lot easier!

━━━━━━━━━━━━ ➔ ACTION ITEM ◆ ━━━━━━━━━

If you need to start now to keep track of your monthly expenses, use the Monthly Expense Record in Figure 20–1. Follow through for at least 3 months, to be sure you aren't overlooking any expenses.

━━━━━━━━━━━━━━━━━━━━━━━━━━━━━━━━━━

With a good record of past expenses, you're ready to start projecting for your future retirement. Take a look at Figure 20–2, your worksheet for estimating retirement expenses.

SAY "GOOD-BYE" TO SOME EXPENSES

In retirement, your expenses may change. Work-related expenses may drop considerably. Your auto expenses will go down if you had been driving to work each day. You'll avoid the costs of work-related clothing, lunches, office donations, and office party contributions. You may no longer have expenses for continuing education, professional journals, and similar commitments.

A second major change could be your housing costs. Many people plan to move to a different home or community or region in retirement. If you sell your home, you may have more money to invest. Your income will go up accordingly.

Selling your home and "buying down" to a retirement home is a big personal decision and an important tax decision as well.

━━━━━━━━━━━━ ➔ ACTION ITEM ◆ ━━━━━━━━━

What plans do you have for moving after you retire? Begin now on your research into retirement housing. Here are some initial financial and tax questions to answer, if you expect to sell your current house:

▶ **Can I take the once-in-a-lifetime $125,000 exclusion on capital gains (personal residence only)?**

▶ **Where do I find the right professional help to fix up, market, and sell my home?**

▶ **When must I buy my retirement home, to be sure I don't pay any more taxes than necessary? (The issue here is "carryforward of basis.")**

▶ **Can I transfer my property tax basis, or defer paying property taxes?**

Answers to these questions require detailed and very special knowledge. Ask your tax preparer, as a first step in getting answers.

SAY "HELLO" TO NEW EXPENSES

Most retirees put travel high on their wish list. Even the costs of local tours add up, in terms of gas, car maintenance, and restaurant meals!

You may not be planning to travel in retirement, but moving to a different community may add new travel expenses as you continue to visit relatives and friends.

Other plans for your newfound leisure may include going back to school (watch for discounts for retired citizens), or home repair or renovation, or putting more time (and money) into a favorite hobby. Spend time estimating home repair costs, or hobbies, or whatever you have planned.

Health insurance may be a new expense. Even if you have the opportunity to continue group coverage through your employer, you will very likely have to pay some of the premium yourself. If you are depending on Medicare for health insurance, be aware that, overall, less than 50 percent of health costs are covered by Medicare. You should consider paying for a good MEDIGAP policy. Additionally, some retirees find long-term or convalescent health care insurance appropriate.

Costs for insurance will not be trivial.

➝ **ACTION ITEM** ◀

Start a file for collecting information regarding your health insurance in retirement. It should include details on:

▶ **The coverage you can expect from your employer**

▶ **Medicare**

▶ **MEDIGAP policies**

▶ **Long-term or convalescent health care**

▶ **Where one coverage begins and another leaves off.**

If you are planning to move to a retirement community, include details of any available medical coverage or assistance offered through the community. This information will probably change regularly. Keep your file up-to-date!

A good source of information on insurance for retirees is the American Association of Retired Persons (AARP). Contact them for a membership (only $5 a year) by writing to AARP, 1909 K Street, N.W., Washington, DC 20049.

ESTIMATE YOUR EXPENSES

Whenever anyone projects living expenses, they are never 100 percent correct. The idea is not necessarily to be completely accurate; just try to get *an idea* of what your expenses will look like. With a good estimate, you can start playing the "what if" games in chapter 21.

--------------- **POINTS TO REMEMBER** ---------------

▶ If you aren't confident that you can estimate your retirement expenses, begin now to keep track on a monthly basis. With a good record of past expenses, you'll be ready to start projecting for your retirement.

▶ Expenses that might go down in retirement include work-related costs and housing.

▶ Expenses that might go up in retirement include travel, hobbies, health insurance, and housing.

▶ You may not be able to project accurately, but an honest attempt will be better than none at all.

21

Long-Range Planning

*T*his chapter describes different retirement planning techniques that will give you an understanding of the long-term implications of decisions you make today. Specific instructions help you combine your worksheets, do simple projections, and, finally, build a long-range planning spreadsheet.

The chapter will increase your awareness, help you avoid mistakes, and give you a sense of the *relative importance* of each of your decisions. It will *not* give you specific answers to all your financial questions!

In our experience, there are seldom easy answers. Occasionally, there is no answer at all, but, in the *process* of examining your retirement financial picture, you will satisfy yourself that you have done the best job possible. A *failure* to plan could be more costly, both financially and emotionally, than a retirement plan that isn't perfectly accurate.

Use our simple techniques, follow the examples, and become your own financial adviser!

COMPARING INCOME TO EXPENSES

To begin, you'll need to compare your income to your expenses, month by month. Use the worksheets in Chapters 18 and 20 to compile this information. From your monthly figures, determine your income and your expenses for the year, and compare those figures.

You may see that, in some months, your income will be greater than your expenses. There may also be times when your expenses are greater than your income. With some planning and control over expenses, everything should work out by the end of the year. All that's required is having a "reserve fund" to fill in the gaps.

What if your expenses *are* greater than your income during your first year or two of retirement? Your first thought may be, "I guess that means I can't retire."

This conclusion may not be accurate.

Some people are wealthy enough to spend more than they bring in for years, and never run out of money. Other people can spend more than they bring in *from time to time* and still not jeopardize their security. Realistically, some people can't retire because their expenses are more than their income and they don't have enough savings to make up the difference.

During the first year or so of retirement, expenses are often higher as retirees enjoy extended traveling, fixing up the house, club membership, or just taking advantage of newfound freedom!

Here's when the long-range version of your plan becomes important.

LONG-RANGE RETIREMENT PLANNING

From the previous chapters, you have identified the categories of information that go into your long-range plan. Now, you must extend your basic numbers to cover a longer time period.

For the sake of simplicity, let's switch from monthly to yearly figures. Table 21–1 is an example of a simple long-range plan.

WEALTH *A Shaky Start.* Rob and Kay have decided on an
BUILDING early retirement—next year, when Rob is 60. They
PROFILE have several extensive trips planned, but expect to cut
back on other spending. They know things will be tight in the first few years, but count on social security to give them some breathing room later on.

If we put together income and expense information about Rob and Kay, we can see their budget and a simplified picture of their situation. Notice that Rob and Kay start their retirement by spending more than they bring in.

Table 21–1 shows their budget figures. Their 5-year plan is diagrammed in Figure 21–1.

Table 21-1
Budget Figures

	Years				
	1	*2*	*3*	*4*	*5*
Income					
Salary[1]	$ 40,000	$20,000	—	—	—
Pension[2]	—	6,000	$ 12,000	$12,000	$12,000
Social security[3]	—	—	—	10,800	11,200
Investments	$ 1,000	$ 2,000	$ 2,000	$ 2,000	$ 2,000
Total income	$ 41,000	$28,000	$ 14,000	$24,800	$25,200
Expenses					
Regular[4]	$ 27,000	$22,000	$ 22,800	$23,800	$24,700
Trips	—	7,000	5,000	—	—
Total expenses	$ 27,000	$29,000	$ 27,800	$23,800	$24,700
Bottom Line	$+14,000	$−1,000	$−13,000	$+1,000	$ +500

[1] Salary continues 6 months into second year.
[2] Pension starts midway during year; no COLA.
[3] Family benefit, reduced to age 62; COLA.
[4] Adjusted upward by inflation.

→ ACTION ITEM ←

Create a simple income and expense chart for the first 5 years of your retirement. Include extraordinary expenses like trips, a car, and so on, as well as regular retirement expenses. Are you spending more than you bring in?

LONGER RANGE PLANNING

Construction of the type of chart shown in Figure 21-1 is not too difficult. The problem is that it shows only 5 years, and you surely plan to live a lot longer than that!

What longer range planning does is show the effect, over time, of negative cash flow, inflation, various investment returns, cost-of-living adjustments (or lack thereof), extra expenses, or changes in life style (such as one spouse being widowed).

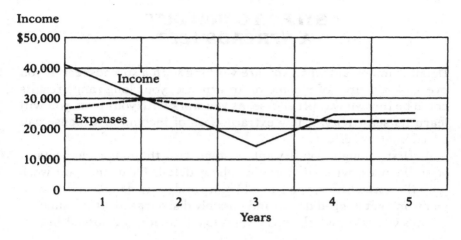

Figure 21-1
Rob and Kay's 5-year plan.

You can't possibly predict inflation, investment returns, or any of the other variables. Still, you can make some pretty good guesses. More than that, you can build plans showing *a whole range* of inflation or investment rates, if you like. Reality will probably be somewhere in the middle.

This is really the strength of a longer range plan—the chance to look at a variety of "what if" happenings.

COMPUTERS, CALCULATORS, AND SPREADSHEETS

Computers are wonderful tools. If you can use one, you'll be able to create a very flexible plan and will have the ability to analyze options quickly. But having a computer is not a necessity. You can make a spreadsheet using a simple calculator.

On a spreadsheet, income and expense amounts are laid out in rows and columns. There are other ways to plan long-range, but we've found the spreadsheet approach to be simple enough, yet complete enough, to suit nearly everyone.

STEPS TO BUILDING
A SPREADSHEET

Detail is important when you are working with a spreadsheet. If you overlook a source of income or an expense, your long-range results could be thrown way off course. As you work with your plan, you will learn its sensitivity. A few extra dollars of income or expense can have long-term effects.

At first, though, you'll want to start with the major elements of your finances, without worrying about detail. Each time you work with the spreadsheet, you can add more and more detail. In that way, you won't get bogged down, and possibly discouraged, at the start.

Let's walk through the basic steps to constructing a spreadsheet.

1. List Your Assets

Make a list of all of your assets (the things you own, including investments, your home, and so on), using the Net Worth Statement shown in Figure 21–2. The Net Worth Statement is a snapshot of your assets, with their values all listed *as of a certain date*. You may wish to make one Net Worth Statement (actual) for this year, and another (a projection) for the year of your retirement, showing what you expect to be worth then.

Figure 21–2(a) is the filled-in Net Worth Statement for John and Marie Sample. Study it for guidance when you fill in your own Net Worth Statement. Figure 21–2(b) is a blank form for your use.

2. Make Assumptions

Refer to Table 21–2, the Sample family's long-range plan, as you move through this step. (We have not provided you with a blank spreadsheet, because your circumstances will be unique.) You may wish to shop at a stationery store for graph paper or an accounting pad, or to create your own long-range plan on plain paper or on a computer.

Begin by making your assumptions for the spreadsheet.

Estimate how the value of your home is going up, the rate of return you expect on investments, and the impact of inflation on your living expenses. All of these are variables that will change, but you need to start somewhere.

Net Worth Statement: John and Marie Sample   Date ___12/31___

	Value	Title	Notes
Personal Assets			
Home (current value)	$ 150,000	_____	_____
Furniture	25,000	_____	_____
Cars	7,000	_____	_____
Collections	—	_____	_____
Other	—	_____	_____
Retirement Plans			
Pension/Profit-sharing			$ 12,000/yr.
401(k)	_____	_____	_____
IRAs	20,000	_____	_____
TSAs	_____	_____	_____
Other	_____	_____	_____
Fixed Assets			
Checking	1,000	_____	_____
Money market funds	4,000	_____	_____
Savings accounts			
#1 Bank A % 5	4,000	_____	_____
#2 Bank B % 6	6,000	_____	_____
Certificates of Deposit			
#1 Bank C % 9 (due 9/92)	60,000	_____	_____
Money owed you	_____	_____	_____
Savings bonds (face)	_____	_____	_____
Deferred annuities	_____	_____	_____
Life insurance cash value	_____	_____	_____
Variable Assets			
Stocks	_____	_____	_____
Bonds	_____	_____	_____
Mutual funds	5,000	_____	_____
Rental real estate (equity)	_____	_____	_____
Hard assets	_____	_____	_____
Other	_____	_____	_____
TOTAL ASSETS	$ 282,000		
Liabilities			
Debt on residence			
#1 Fed. 1st % 8 date '58	$ 5,000		
#2 _____ % ___ date ___	_____		
Car loan %_____	_____		
Other	_____		
TOTAL LIABILITIES	$ 5,000		
NET WORTH (Assets less liabilities)	$ 277,000		
Add value of life insurance for TOTAL ESTATE	_____		

————————————— **Figure 21.2(a)** —————————————
Comprehensive Net Worth Statement.

Net Worth Statement: Date _____

	Value	Title	Notes
Personal Assets			
Home (current value)			
Furniture			
Cars			
Collections			
Other			
Retirement Plans			
Pension/Profit-sharing			
401(k)			
IRAs			
TSAs			
Other			
Fixed Assets			
Checking			
Money market funds			
Savings accounts			
#1 _____ %____			
#2 _____ %____			
Certificates of Deposit			
#1 _____ %____ (due ____)			
Money owed you			
Savings bonds (face)			
Deferred annuities			
Life insurance cash value			
Variable Assets			
Stocks			
Bonds			
Mutual funds			
Rental real estate (equity)			
Hard assets			
Other			
TOTAL ASSETS			
Liabilities			
Debt on residence			
#1 _____ %____ date ____			
#2 _____ %____ date ____			
Car loan %_____			
Other			
TOTAL LIABILITIES			
NET WORTH (Assets less liabilities)			
Add value of life insurance for TOTAL ESTATE			

─────────── **Figure 21.2(b)** ───────────

Form for comprehensive Net Worth Statement.

▶ I expect my home to increase in value _____ percent each year.

▶ I expect my living expenses to increase _____ percent each year.

▶ On average, I believe I can receive _____ percent return on my investments each year.

Keep in mind that some expenses won't adjust with inflation—a car payment or a fixed interest mortgage payment, for example. Eventually, these expenses will be paid off, and they won't appear any more among your annual expenses.

If your expenses are not relatively constant each year, you may want to lay them out in great detail, showing amounts and dates when estimated expenses are to be paid. This entails some guesswork, but, as you work with your numbers, your estimates will become more accurate. When in doubt, always leave a safety margin.

3. Estimate Income

Using your benefits statement and the information contained within this book, estimate your retirement plan income and social security.

▶ From my retirement plan(s) I expect to receive, each year, $_____.

▶ This income will continue until I am age _____.

▶ I expect my retirement plan benefit to increase _____ percent each year.

▶ I expect to receive from social security $_____.

▶ Social security will begin when I am age _____.

▶ I expect social security to increase _____ percent each year.

Social security has a cost-of-living adjustment (COLA) built in. You may wish to use 2 or 3 percent as a conservative starting figure for the COLA.

4. Identify Your Time Frame

When you identify your time frame, you may start with this year, or you may want to start with the first year of your retirement. Down the left side of the page, make a column of the years the spreadsheet will

Table 21-2

Year	Asset Base		Sources	
	Residence Investment Capital		Yield from	Pension
	Nonliquid	Liquid	Investments	Income
1	$150,000	$100,000	$6,000	$12,000
2	$157,500	$107,000	$6,420	$12,000
3	$165,375	$113,530	$6,812	$12,000
4	$173,644	$119,510	$7,171	$12,000
5	$182,326	$124,853	$7,491	$12,000
6	$191,442	$129,462	$7,768	$12,000
7	$201,014	$133,234	$7,994	$12,000
8	$211,065	$136,055	$8,163	$12,000
9	$221,618	$137,799	$8,268	$12,000
10	$232,699	$138,332	$8,300	$12,000
11	$244,334	$137,506	$8,250	$12,000
12	$256,551	$135,161	$8,110	$12,000
13	$269,378	$131,123	$7,867	$12,000
14	$282,847	$125,203	$7,512	$12,000
15	$296,990	$117,196	$7,032	$12,000
16	$311,839	$106,881	$6,413	$12,000
17	$327,431	$94,016	$5,641	$12,000
18	$343,803	$78,341	$4,700	$12,000
19	$360,993	$59,576	$3,575	$12,000
20	$379,043	$37,414	$2,245	$12,000

Sample Retirement Spreadsheet
Prepared for
John and Marie Sample

Assumptions:

Investment Capital	$100,000
Pre-tax Return	6%
Social Security	$ 12,000
Social Security Index	3%
Pension	$ 12,000
Pension Index	0%
IRA	$ 20,000
Annual Expenses	$ 25,000
Inflation	5%
Residence	$150,000
Residence Index	5%

of Income			Expenses	
IRA Withdrawal	Social Security	Total Income	Annual Expenses Including Taxes	Net Liquid Asset Change
$2,000	$12,000	$32,000	$25,000	$7,000
$2,000	$12,360	$32,780	$26,250	$6,530
$2,000	$12,731	$33,543	$27,563	$5,980
$2,000	$13,113	$34,283	$28,941	$5,343
$2,000	$13,506	$34,997	$30,388	$4,610
$2,000	$13,911	$35,679	$31,907	$3,772
$2,000	$14,329	$36,323	$33,502	$2,820
$2,000	$14,758	$36,922	$35,178	$1,744
$2,000	$15,201	$37,469	$36,936	$533
$2,000	$15,657	$37,957	$38,783	($826)
$2,000	$16,127	$38,377	$40,722	($2,345)
$2,000	$16,611	$38,720	$42,758	($4,038)
$2,000	$17,109	$38,976	$44,896	($5,920)
$2,000	$17,622	$39,135	$47,141	($8,007)
$2,000	$18,151	$39,183	$49,498	($10,315)
$2,000	$18,696	$39,108	$51,973	($12,865)
$2,000	$19,256	$38,897	$54,572	($15,674)
$2,000	$19,834	$38,535	$57,300	($18,766)
$2,000	$20,429	$38,004	$60,165	($22,162)
$2,000	$21,042	$37,287	$63,174	($25,887)

cover. Beside the years, put your age(s). As you know, age can trigger certain retirement events, such as starting Medicare, beginning withdrawals from your IRA, and so on.

5. Title Columns

Across the top of the page, title the columns. Set up three major categories: your assets, your sources of income, and your expenses. Nonliquid assets are assets you can't readily cash in, such as your house. They may or may not be sources of income, but they are still assets. Liquid assets are savings accounts, mutual funds, stocks, and so on. In our example, for simplicity, we have lumped all the liquid assets together under the title Investment Capital. In reality, you may want to list each major asset separately. Investment income is the interest and dividends you earn from your investments.

Income and expense figures can be transferred from your worksheets.

6. Calculate Year 1

Going across the first row, add up all sources of income, subtract expenses, and show your profit or loss in the Net column. This is the amount you are ahead (or behind) when the year ends.

7. Adjust for Each Year

If you are ahead at the end of the year, you didn't spend all the income that came in. You'll be able to put that extra income into a savings account, where it can earn interest for you for the next year. In our example, the profit from the previous year is added to the Investment Capital account.

If you are behind at year-end, you spent more money than came in. Your loss must be subtracted from the Investment Capital account. This subtraction adjusts the assets for the next year.

Continue this way with each year on the spreadsheet. Plug in new sources of income (capital gains, inheritance, and so on) in the year you expect to receive them. By the same token, don't forget special expenses such as trips or cars, which need to be included in the expense column in their particular year. The spreadsheet is flexible enough to meet your specific needs.

PLANNING YOUR RETIREMENT

Planning for a successful retirement is not simple. It takes dedication, perseverance, and plain hard work. We hope your task will be easier because of the questions, suggestions, and tools we've put into this book. By using them all, you can join the ranks of the retirement planning experts.

We wish you the best of luck!

What are the key points to look for on a spreadsheet?

You'll notice right away whether you are ahead or behind in any given year. Watch for any year in which you begin to subtract from the Investment Capital account to make ends meet. (This is called, ominously, "invasion of capital!")

If you subtract from your capital each year, you will be depleting or closing out accounts. You may also have to sell assets. The spreadsheet will help you determine when you might have to sell such assets as stock or real estate. Plan early for these sales, because they may take a while to accomplish.

How long will my assets last?

In our illustration, subtraction from the Investment Capital account began in year 11. Figure 21–3 shows how the Samples' Investment Capital account builds up, then begins to decline in value over the course of their long-range plan.

Even with the decline, it looks as though the Samples' investment assets will last many more years.

At one point, the residence could be sold. As long as the Samples buy a less expensive house, they will have extra money to replenish their Investment Capital account.

Your long-range plan may resemble the Samples' plan, or it may be very different. Like theirs, your plan will never be perfectly accurate, but you will certainly see whether you are "on the right track" with your long-range planning spreadsheet.

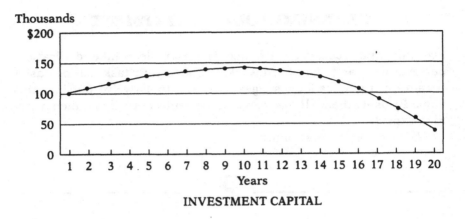

INVESTMENT CAPITAL

—————————— **Figure 21–3** ——————————
Sample retirement analysis: John and Marie Sample.

What different scenarios should I look at?

If your retirement planning isn't working as you had hoped, you can adjust it to see the impact of:

▶ Working another year or two before retiring

▶ Delaying or advancing income from social security

▶ Advancing or delaying IRA distributions

▶ Selling your personal residence and buying a less expensive home

▶ Working part-time in retirement

▶ Cutting back expenses.

The above variations originate from decisions you can control. There will be other events that you can't influence. That's why you should play "what-if" games that focus on:

▶ Higher or lower inflation rates

▶ Better or worse return on investments or cost-of-living adjustments

▶ Each half of a couple surviving alone.

Remember, your spreadsheet is based on your assumptions. As your assumptions change, your spreadsheet must be reworked.

→ ACTION ITEM ←

Build a long-range plan using the spreadsheet format. Create several versions showing a best case, an expected case, and a worst case. Play with the spreadsheet to get familiar with the long-range impact of changes. Update your spreadsheet regularly as you get new information. With your spreadsheet, you'll be heading for a confident retirement!

POINTS TO REMEMBER

▸ There are seldom easy answers to financial questions regarding retirement. Occasionally, there is no answer at all. But in the *process* of examining your retirement financial picture, you will satisfy yourself that you have done the best job possible.

▸ Start by creating a simple Income and Expense Chart for the first 5 years of your retirement.

▸ Then extend your planning for 20 or 30 years, using multiple "what-if" scenarios to account for variations in inflation, investment return, and family circumstances.

▸ The spreadsheet approach to long-range planning is simple enough, yet complete enough, to suit nearly everyone.

Appendix: Finding and Using a Professional Adviser

WHERE TO START

Finding a qualified adviser is no easy task. Plenty of people will try to help, but you want the person who *can* help. Your first step is to define the problem.

Write the problem down. Force yourself to describe it in a few key sentences. With this definition in hand, go to your "inner circle" of advisers: your benefits representative, insurance broker, tax preparer, attorney, or financial planner. If you haven't used these people before, ask friends and relatives for referrals.

Start by viewing the description you've written of your problem. Ask whether you are expressing it accurately. Have you described it in enough detail? Is it a true concern?

> Once the problem is clearly defined, there is a good chance you (or your inner circle of advisers) may solve it readily!

If your problem can't be solved at this level, your adviser will refer you to a specialist. (A real professional will admit he or she can't solve every case.) Get at least two or three names.

Call the specialists and interview them over the phone.

THE TELEPHONE INTERVIEW

In the telephone interview, find out as much as you can about the specialists: background, education, certification, and special experience related to your problem. Ask about fees and contracts; be sure you understand how the specialist will be paid for the time he or she is spending with you. (Remember the "no free lunch" principle.)

The specialists will want information about you and your problem. Be prepared with amounts, dates, and other details. You won't have to educate a qualified specialist. He or she should quickly grasp the issue and know how to get answers.

Decide which specialist appears capable and interested in handling your problem. Don't hesitate to consider your "gut feeling" in making this choice; you are likely to get further faster with someone you find compatible.

Set an appointment, usually at the specialist's office. Ask about any special information you need to bring, such as income tax returns, benefits books or statements, wills or trusts, and so on. Often, the specialist will send a letter detailing how to prepare for the meeting.

THE APPOINTMENT

Prior to the appointment, the specialist will usually send you personal data sheets to be filled out. Much of the information requested will be the information you have been dealing with in this book.

Don't withhold any information on these forms. Many issues are complex and interrelated. What you consider trivial or unimportant may make or break a decision!

If you feel you need to bring out detailed background information, you may wish to mail it ahead of time.

At the appointment, the specialist will control the discussion by using questions to get to the important issues. Answer the questions directly. Try not to bring in all aspects of the problem with every answer you give. A good interviewer will ask the important questions and take notes; you won't have to repeat yourself.

At the end of the appointment, the specialist may not have an answer to your problem. Discuss how much more time it may take. Be sure to ask for a breakdown of rates, fees, and billing procedure. (Will an aide, at a lower hourly cost, be doing most of the research?) To reduce cost, offer to do some of the "legwork" yourself, such as writing letters or tracking down information.

Set up a second appointment before you leave. This will help you put a time frame around your problem; you'll also know when to check on progress.

By the end of the second appointment, if the specialist hasn't offered a solution to your problem, determine whether it is going to be solved within a reasonable time. You must decide what is reasonable. If it can't be solved within your time frame, consider finding another specialist.

SECOND OPINION

Once you think you have *the* answer, don't be afraid to get a second opinion. By now, you will have gathered all the information, so a confirmation of your decision should be easy to get. Expect to pay for this second opinion, even if it doesn't take much time.

TAX ISSUES

Under current tax law, the fee you pay a specialist for retirement advice is a personal expense and is not deductible. If the discussion is clearly related to income tax planning, it may be deductible. Be sure to ask your adviser to indicate on your bill which advice is income tax-related.

Afterword

We have not succeeded in answering all of our questions; indeed, we have not completely answered any of them. The answers we have found have only served to raise a whole new set of questions. In most ways, we feel we are as confused as ever, but we think we are confused on a much higher level about much more important things.

Anonymous

Index